NIST Special Publication 800-152

A Profile for U.S. Federal Cryptographic Key Management Systems

Elaine Barker
Miles Smid
Dennis Branstad

This publication is available free of charge from:
http://dx.doi.org/10.6028/NIST.SP.800-152

COMPUTER SECURITY

National Institute of
Standards and Technology
U.S. Department of Commerce

NIST Special Publication 800-152

A Profile for U. S. Federal Cryptographic Key Management Systems

Elaine Barker
Computer Security Division
Information Technology Laboratory

Miles Smid
G2, Inc.
Annapolis Junction, MD

Dennis Branstad
NIST Consultant
Austin, TX

This publication is available free of charge from:
http://dx.doi.org/10.6028/NIST.SP.800-152

October 2015

U.S. Department of Commerce
Penny Pritzker, Secretary

National Institute of Standards and Technology
Willie May, Under Secretary of Commerce for Standards and Technology and Director

Authority

This publication has been developed by NIST to further its statutory responsibility under the Federal Information Security Modernization Act (FISMA) of 2014, 44 U.S.C. § 3541 *et seq.*, Public Law (P.L.) 113-283. NIST is responsible for developing information-security standards and guidelines, including minimum requirements for Federal information systems, but such standards and guidelines shall not apply to national security systems without the express approval of appropriate Federal officials exercising policy authority over such systems. This guideline is consistent with the requirements of the Office of Management and Budget (OMB) Circular A-130.

Nothing in this publication should be taken to contradict the standards and guidelines made mandatory and binding on Federal agencies by the Secretary of Commerce under statutory authority. Nor should these guidelines be interpreted as altering or superseding the existing authorities of the Secretary of Commerce, Director of the OMB, or any other Federal official. This publication may be used by nongovernmental organizations on a voluntary basis and is not subject to copyright in the United States. Attribution would, however, be appreciated by NIST.

National Institute of Standards and Technology Special Publication 800-152
Natl. Inst. Stand. Technol. Spec. Publ. 800-152, 146 pages (October 2015)
CODEN: NSPUE2

This publication is available free of charge from:
http://dx.doi.org/10.6028/NIST.SP.800-152

Comments on this publication may be submitted to:

National Institute of Standards and Technology
Attn: Computer Security Division, Information Technology Laboratory
100 Bureau Drive (Mail Stop 8930) Gaithersburg, MD 20899-8930
Email: FederalCKMSProfile@nist.gov

Reports on Computer Systems Technology

The Information Technology Laboratory (ITL) at the National Institute of Standards and Technology (NIST) promotes the U.S. economy and public welfare by providing technical leadership for the Nation's measurement and standards infrastructure. ITL develops tests, test methods, reference data, proof-of-concept implementations, and technical analyses to advance the development and productive use of information technology. ITL's responsibilities include the development of management, administrative, technical, and physical standards and guidelines for the cost-effective security and privacy of other than national security-related information in federal information systems. The Special Publication 800-series reports on ITL's research, guidelines, and outreach efforts in information system security, and its collaborative activities with industry, government, and academic organizations.

Abstract

This Profile for U. S. Federal Cryptographic Key Management Systems (FCKMSs) contains requirements for their design, implementation, procurement, installation, configuration, management, operation, and use by U. S. Federal organizations. The Profile is based on NIST Special Publication (SP) 800-130, *A Framework for Designing Cryptographic Key Management Systems (CKMS)*.

Keywords

access control; confidentiality; cryptographic key management system; disaster recovery; federal cryptographic key management system; integrity; metadata; security assessment; security functions; security policies; source authentication.

Acknowledgements

The National Institute of Standards and Technology (NIST) acknowledges and greatly appreciates contributions by all those who participated in the creation, review, and publication of this document. NIST also thanks the many public and private sector contributors whose constructive comments significantly improved its quality and usefulness. Many useful suggestions on Cryptographic Key Management that were made during the workshops held at NIST in 2009, 2010, 2012, and 2014 have been incorporated into this document.

Executive Summary

The National Institute of Standards and Technology (NIST) Cryptographic Key Management project covers major aspects of managing the cryptographic keys that protect sensitive, unclassified federal information. Associated with each key is specific information (e.g., the identifier associated with its owner, its length, and acceptable uses) called metadata. The computers, software, modules, communications, and roles assumed by one or more authorized individuals when managing and using cryptographic key management services are collectively called a Cryptographic Key Management System (CKMS).

This Profile for U. S. Federal Cryptographic Key Management Systems (FCKMSs) has been prepared to assist CKMS designers and implementers in selecting the features to be provided in their "products," and to assist federal organizations and their contractors when procuring, installing, configuring, operating, and using FCKMSs. Other organizations may use this Profile as desired.

An FCKMS can be owned and operated by a federal organization or by a private contractor that provides key management services for federal organizations or other contractors performing federal information-processing services.

This Profile can also be used by agencies and organizations to understand their FCKMSs, and to adopt, adapt and migrate their FCKMSs to comply with the Profile requirements over time. NIST does not expect that these requirements would be implemented immediately, but that agencies would use these requirements when creating or procuring FCKMSs or FCKMS services for their Enterprise Architectures.

This Profile is based on NIST Special Publication 800-130, *A Framework for Designing Cryptographic Key Management Systems*. The Framework specifies topics that should be considered by a CKMS designer when selecting the capabilities that a CKMS will have and the cryptographic key management services it will support. This Profile replicates all of the Framework requirements that must be satisfied in a CKMS and its design documentation, and includes additional information about installing, configuring, operating and maintaining an FCKMS.

The Framework and this Profile could be used by other organizations that have security requirements similar to those specified in these documents or could be used as a model for the development of other profiles.

Table of Contents

List of Figures

1 Introduction

This *Profile for U.S. Federal Cryptographic Key Management Systems* (FCKMSs[1]) is based on [SP 800-130], entitled "*A Framework for Designing Cryptographic Key Management Systems (CKMS)*," which provides a foundation for designing and implementing CKMSs. The Framework specifies requirements for designing any commercial or Federal CKMS, while this Profile provides more-specific design requirements for an FCKMS, and includes additional requirements for testing, procuring, installing, managing, operating, maintaining, and using FCKMSs.

This Profile specifies requirements for all FCKMSs. It is intended to assist CKMS designers and implementers to select and support appropriate security services and key-management functions, and to assist FCKMS procurers, administrators, service-providing organizations, and service-using organizations to select appropriate CKMSs or CKMS services. This Profile specifies requirements for all organizations desiring to operate or use an FCKMS, either directly or under contract; makes recommendations for Federal organizations having special security needs and desiring to augment the base security and key-management services; and suggests additional FCKMS features that may be desirable for Federal organizations to implement and use now or in the future

This Profile can be used by agencies and organizations to understand their FCKMSs, and to adopt, adapt and migrate their FCKMSs to comply with the Profile requirements over time. NIST does not expect that these requirements would be implemented immediately, but that agencies would use these requirements when creating or procuring FCKMSs or FCKMS services for their Enterprise Architectures. Agencies can also use these requirements to assess and understand potential gaps that exist in their current FCKMSs. As agencies plan for changes, migrations and upgrades, these requirements and the gap assessment can be used to improve the security of FCKMs overall.

This Profile is intended to:

1. Assist CKMS designers and implementers in supporting appropriate key and metadata management functions, cryptographic key types, key metadata, and protocols for protecting sensitive U.S. Federal computing applications and data;

2. Establish requirements for FCKMS testing, procurement, installation, configuration, administration, operation, maintenance and usage;

3. Facilitate an easy comparison of one FCKMS with another by analyzing their designs and implementations in order to understand how each meets the Framework and Profile requirements; and

4. Assist in understanding what is needed to evaluate, procure, install, configure, administer, operate, and use an FCKMS that manages the cryptographic keys that protect sensitive and valuable data obtained, processed, stored, and used by U.S. Federal organizations and their contractors.

---

[1] A CKMS is intended to be the system designed and built by a CKMS designer and implementer, while an FCKMS is the system used by the Federal government, after the CKMS has been designed and configured to be compliant with Federal needs.

5. Assist Agencies in performing an initial assessment of their FCKMSs to clearly understand where potential gap areas might exist, where there are areas for potential improvements and to understand requirements for future migrations, procurements and upgrades to their FCKMSs.

Designing a secure CKMS is the responsibility of CKMS designers, who must choose among various key-management capabilities to be included in a product being designed for a particular market. Purchasing an acceptable FCKMS or FCKMS service is the responsibility of Federal procurement officials and their technical associates. Managing/administering an FCKMS is the responsibility of appropriate FCKMS service providers when installing, configuring, operating, and maintaining an FCKMS.

This Profile is based on the Framework, and readers of this Profile are strongly encouraged to be familiar with the information in the Framework. The Framework contains tutorial information that may be needed to understand the cryptographic key-management topics of this Profile. This Profile introduces each topic that is also covered in the Framework.

The Framework and this Profile could be used by other organizations that have security requirements similar to those specified in these documents, and the Profile could be used as a model for the development of other profiles.

1.1   Profile Terminology

The Profile often uses terminology that is not used in the Framework. A glossary of terms is provided in Appendix B, but some of the more general terms merit an introduction below.

"CKMS" is used to mean any Cryptographic Key Management System that satisfies the requirements of the Framework. The term refers to the system that is designed and implemented, possibly with configurable options.

An "FCKMS" performs the key and metadata functions that are the foundation of all cryptographic key-management services needed by one or more Federal service-using organizations and their employees.

An FCKMS includes a CKMS, possibly after configuring the CKMS functions to support the desired services of a Federal service-using organization. An FCKMS also meets all the requirements of this Profile for its impact-level and provides FCKMS services for a U.S. Federal organization and/or its contractors.

This Profile uses the terms "FCKMS service-providing organization" (or "FCKMS service provider") and "FCKMS service-using organization". An FCKMS service provider may be a part of an FCKMS service-using organization or may be an independent organization providing the services required by FCKMS service-using organizations (e.g., under contract). Federal CKMS service providers may be Federal organizations, Federal contractors, or both. This Profile includes requirements for both FCKMS service providers and FCKMS service-using organizations.

This Profile uses the term "impact-level" to refer to the information-system impact-levels identified in [FIPS 200]. [FIPS 200] uses the security categories in [FIPS 199] to specify and define three information-system impact-levels: Low, Moderate and High. The security categories are based on the potential impact on an organization if certain events occur that jeopardize the information and information systems needed by the organization to accomplish its assigned mission, protect its assets, fulfill its legal responsibilities, maintain its day-to-day functions, and protect individuals.

The Profile uses the term "security control" to refer to the security controls provided in [SP 800-53] that support the executive agencies of the Federal government to meet the requirements of [FIPS 200]. [SP 800-53], and [SP 800-53A] apply to all components of an information system that process, store, or transmit Federal information.

The term "FIPS-140 security level" refers to the security levels defined for cryptographic modules in [FIPS 140]. Four levels are defined, where a level 1 cryptographic module provides the least amount of protection, and a level 4 module provides the greatest amount of protection. The cryptographic modules and their implemented FIPS-140 security levels are validated by NIST's Cryptographic Module Validation Program (CMVP).

The term "security strength" is used to measure the amount of cryptographic protection that can be provided by a combination of a cryptographic algorithm and a key. Further discussion of key strengths is provided in [SP 800-57 Part 1].

In CKMS and FCKMS topic discussions, statements of fact are indicated by "is" or "are"; statements of permission or of possibility are indicated by "may"; statements of capability are indicated by "can". Statements including "could" are used in discussing possible optional or alternative actions. These terms do not indicate requirements or recommendations of this publication.

1.2 Scope of this Profile

An FCKMS is intended for use by Federal agencies and contractors (who use cryptography to protect U.S. government information) to manage all the cryptographic keys and associated metadata.

While individual people are outside the scope of an FCKMS, the roles assumed by these people (e.g., administrators, managers, operators, auditors, and users) are within the scope of an FCKMS. Physical and logical interfaces between an FCKMS and any or all these roles are also within an FCKMS's scope.

Federal agencies and their contractors are required to select appropriate [FIPS 199] impact levels for their information and to select security controls from those identified in [SP 800-53] to use in procurements, implementations and planning. After selecting the applicable security control(s), organizations can initiate the tailoring process to appropriately modify and align the controls more closely with the specific conditions within the organization (i.e., conditions related to organizational missions/business functions, information systems, or environments of operation). This Profile addresses the selection of several of the security controls specified in [SP 800-53], indicating the minimum requirements for those security controls for each impact level. Other security controls not specifically addressed herein should be selected as appropriate for the organization's systems.

1.3 Audience

This Profile is intended for CKMS designers and implementers, as well as FCKMS procurers, installers, configuration personnel, administrators, managers, operators, and users.

Federal employees and Federal contractors are the anticipated users of the services provided by an FCKMS. Members of the public sector could be authorized to use the services of an FCKMS when interacting with Federal organizations and their contractors.

1.4 Organization

Section 1, **Introduction,** introduces Cryptographic Key Management, CKMSs, FCKMSs, and the Profile.

Section 2, **Profile Basics,** covers the fundamentals of the Profile and an FCKMS.

Section 3, **Goals,** defines the goals of an FCKMS.

Section 4, **Security Policies,** presents the need for and the scope of one or more policies governing the management and use of an FCKMS.

Section 5, **Roles and Responsibilities,** describes various roles and responsibilities of the people managing, operating, and using an FCKMS.

Section 6, **Cryptographic Keys and Metadata,** discusses cryptographic algorithms, keys and metadata, various key and metadata management functions, security issues, and error/damage recovery mechanisms.

Section 7, **Interoperability and Transitioning,** considers the interoperability of FCKMSs and their ability to satisfy future key-management needs.

Section 8, **Security Controls,** describes the security controls used to protect an FCKMS.

Section 9, **Testing and System Assurances,** describes security testing and obtaining assurances that security services are being performed correctly.

Section 10, **Disaster Recovery,** discusses various FCKMS service and data backup capabilities and recovering from several types of disasters.

Section 11, **Security Assessment,** discusses assessing the operation and security of an FCKMS.

Section 12, **Technology Challenges,** discusses the technical advances that could affect the security of an FCKMS.

Appendix A, References, provides relevant information for accessing each publication referenced herein.

Appendix B, Glossary, provides a glossary of terms used in this Profile.

2   Profile Basics

This Profile provides a structured view of a Federal CKMS, discussing security provisions that **shall**, **should** or **could** be used by a Federal organization or contractor to manage and protect cryptographic keys and metadata.

2.1   Profile Topics and Requirements, Augmentations, and Features

This Profile consists of a set of topics that is similar to the topics found in the Framework. Each topic heading is typically followed by an overview of the topic, a list of Framework requirements from [SP 800-130], a list of Profile requirements, a list of recommended Profile augmentations, and a list of possible Profile features. In some cases, there may be no requirements, augmentations, or features that apply to the topic.

Framework requirements for CKMSs are indicated by "**shall**" or "**shall not**," and are numbered beginning with an "**FR**" designation. Profile requirements for all FCKMSs are indicated by "**shall**" or "**shall not**," and are numbered beginning with a "**PR**" designation. Some Profile requirements are conditional (e.g., based on the applicable [FIPS 200] impact-level). Only the Framework requirements and the non-conditional Profile requirements are necessary to conform to and comply with this document. A CKMS design conforming to this Profile, must support a configuration that is compatible with both sets of requirements. Recommended augmentations are indicated by "**should**," and are numbered beginning with a "**PA**" designation. Recommended augmentations are strongly recommended by NIST for implementation in most systems. Possible features are indicated by "**could**," and are numbered beginning with a "**PF**" designation. Profile features are optional features that are often intended for complex or future systems. Their possible implementation, if desired, is left to the stakeholders of the system. Federal CKMS service-using organizations could selectively require that their FCKMSs support some of the recommended augmentations or suggested features, but such requirements are beyond the scope of this document.

In order to easily recognize Profile requirements, augmentations and features from the surrounding text, each type is presented in separate tables. For each table:

- Column one provides the PR, PA or PF number;
- Column two identifies any related security controls in [SP 800-53]; when column two is blank, no related security control has been identified; and
- Column three provides the text of the requirement, augmentation or feature.

The first Framework requirement and the first Profile requirement, recommended augmentation and suggested feature are concerned with the overall conformance to the Framework and Profile.

FR:1.1 A conformant CKMS design **shall** meet all "**shall**" requirements of the Framework [SP 800-130].

PR:2.1		A Federal CKMS **shall** satisfy all Framework requirements (**FRs**) and Profile requirements (**PRs**).

PA:2.1		A Federal CKMS **should** support Profile augmentations (**PAs**).

PF:2.1		A Federal CKMS **could** support Profile features (**PFs**).

2.2 Rationale for Cryptographic Key Management

Today's information systems require protection against the denial of authorized use of their services; unauthorized access to, or modification of, their information processing capabilities; and unauthorized destruction of their equipment and facilities. The information systems themselves must also protect the information that they contain from unauthorized disclosure, modification, and destruction. These protections may be provided by physical means, such as enclosures, locks, and guards, or they can be provided by logical means, such as cryptography or software-based access control.

Cryptography is the only means for protecting data during transmission when physical protection is cost-prohibitive or impossible to provide. Thus, cryptography is widely used when business is conducted or sensitive information is transmitted over a network. Cryptography also provides excellent protection for stored data against entities that are not authorized to obtain or modify the data.

Cryptographic protection for data requires algorithms designed specifically for that purpose. These algorithms often require the use of cryptographic keys, which are managed by an FCKMS. The combination of the cryptographic algorithms and keys of an appropriate length can be used to provide a level of protection for data; this level is commonly referred to as the security strength (see [SP 800-57 Part1] for additional information).

Cryptographic-based security requires the secure management of keys throughout their lifetime. Cryptography can reduce the scope of information management from protecting large amounts of information to protecting a key and its associated metadata (i.e., information about the key). This Profile specifies requirements for the management of the keys used to protect sensitive Federal information and the metadata associated with those keys.

FR:2.1 The CKMS design **shall** specify all cryptographic algorithms and supported key sizes for each algorithm used by the system.

FR:2.2 The CKMS design **shall** specify the estimated security strength of each cryptographic technique that is employed to protect keys and their bound metadata.

Among the initial requirements for this Profile are requirements for the use of NIST-approved cryptography and the minimum security strengths required for each [FIPS 199] impact level.

The current minimum security strength recommended for Federal applications is 112 bits; this minimum has been required for the protection of Low impact-level information and allows the use of a range of algorithms and key lengths commonly in use that provide at least 112 bit of security, including three-key Triple DEA for encryption and 2048-bit RSA.

For Moderate impact-level information, at least128 bits of security is required, which allows, for example, the use of AES-128 for encryption and 3072-bit Diffie-Hellman for key establishment.

While 128 bits of security might also be currently acceptable for most High-level information, it is anticipated that future technology (e.g., quantum computers) will necessitate a higher level of protection for High-impact level information (either 192 or 256 bits of security). This Recommendation requires at least 192 bits of security for the protection of High-impact information in order to align with [Suite B].

PR:2.2	SC-13	A Federal CKMS **shall** support NIST-approved cryptographic algorithms, key-establishment schemes and modes of operation (as needed) in accordance with [SP 800-131A].
PR:2.3		In a Federal CKMS, information (including loaded code and parameters) rated at a Low impact-level **shall** be protected with cryptographic algorithms and keys that provide at least 112 bits of security strength.
PR:2.4		In a Federal CKMS, information (including loaded code and parameters) rated at a Moderate impact-level **shall** be protected with cryptographic algorithms and keys that provide at least 128 bits of security strength.
PR:2.5		In a Federal CKMS, information (including loaded code and parameters) rated at a High impact-level **shall** be protected with cryptographic algorithms and keys that provide at least 192 bits of security strength.

2.3 Keys, Metadata, Trusted Associations, and Bindings

Cryptographic keys are used when applying cryptographic protection to information[2] or processing already-protected information[3]. All keys require integrity protection that should be verified before a key is used. Secret and private keys also require confidentiality protection. Before a key is used, the source of the key should be authenticated.

Information about a cryptographic key that specifies its characteristics, acceptable uses, and applicable parameters must be associated with the key. This information is called the key's metadata, and each descriptive item is called a metadata element. A key and its metadata

---

[2] For example, encrypting plaintext information to protect its confidentiality, or signing the information to protect its integrity and verify its source.

[3] For example, decrypting ciphertext to obtain the original plaintext, or verifying a signature to assure its continued integrity.

must be logically or cryptographically linked together and then protected, either cryptographically or physically. These operations are further discussed in Section 6.4.10.

A metadata element for a key could be implicitly known by the FCKMS, but is often explicitly associated and stored with the key. Some metadata elements are sensitive to unauthorized disclosure and, therefore, require confidentiality protection. Like keys, metadata needs protection against unauthorized modification, and the source should be authenticated before the metadata is used. The amount of protection provided to a key and its metadata should be commensurate with the [FIPS 199] security category and [FIPS 200] information-system impact-level of the data being protected by that key and its metadata.

Keys are considered as being either static or ephemeral. Static keys are typically used multiple times and are considered as being "long-term" keys. Ephemeral keys are usually generated when needed and used only once; they are considered to be "short-term" keys.

A trusted association must be established between each static key and its metadata when they are created by the FCKMS, and this association should be maintained throughout the lifetime of the key. A trusted association can be established by a cryptographic binding between a key and its metadata (e.g., a digital signature computed on a key and its metadata), or by a trusted process (e.g., a face-to-face handover of metadata from an entity who is known and trusted). An FCKMS should provide cryptographic binding and verification functions that are used in the key and metadata distribution and management processes.

2.4　FCKMS Functions

An FCKMS provides key and metadata management functions for cryptographic-based security in user applications, such as secure data communication and storage. These functions include the generation, distribution and destruction of cryptographic keys and their associated metadata (see Section 6.4).

2.5　CKMS Design

In accordance with the Framework, any CKMS design should describe how it provides cryptographic keys to the entities that will use those keys to protect sensitive data. The CKMS design documentation should specify the use of each key type, where and how keys can be generated, how they can be protected in storage and during delivery, and the types of entities to whom they can be delivered.

FR:2.3 A compliant CKMS design **shall** describe design selections and provide documentation as required by the requirements of the Framework.

FR:2.4 The CKMS design **shall** specify a high-level overview of the CKMS system that includes:

a) The use of each key type,
b) Where and how the keys are generated,
c) The metadata elements that are used in a trusted association with each key type,
d) How keys and/or metadata are protected in storage at each entity where they reside,

e) How keys and/or metadata are protected during distribution, and

f) The types of entities to which keys and/or metadata can be delivered (e.g., user, user device, network device).

PR:2.6	SC-12	A Federal CKMS **shall** support the availability and security of its cryptographic keys and their associated metadata.
PR:2.7		A Federal CKMS **shall** be implemented in accordance with the CKMS design that is specified in the CKMS design documentation and support all the specified services, functions, and features of the design.
PR:2.8	SA-5	A Federal CKMS compliance document **shall** be created prior to the initial operation of an FCKMS, describing how each Profile requirement is satisfied and how each implemented augmentation and/or feature is satisfied.

2.6 CKMS Profile

A CKMS Profile provides the requirements that a qualifying CKMS, its implementation, and its operation must meet for a particular sector of interest, such as the Federal government. A CKMS Profile specifies how the CKMS must be designed, implemented, tested, evaluated, and operated. A CKMS Profile is a set of requirements that must be satisfied for a given impact-level by a CKMS as implemented in an operational system.

2.7 FCKMS Profile

This FCKMS Profile (i.e., [SP 800-152]) specifies requirements, augmentations, and features for the U.S. Federal government that will allow a CKMS designer and implementer to create an FCKMS that can be used to protect Federal government information.

2.8 Differences between the Framework and This Profile

In the Framework, this section discusses the differences between a Framework and a profile of that Framework. Essentially, the Framework requires that specific topics be addressed during the design of a CKMS and described in design documentation. Any CKMS complies with the Framework if its design documentation satisfies all the Framework Requirements. A profile states the specific requirements that must be met in order to have a satisfactory CKMS for the designated using sector. This Profile (i.e., SP 800-152) imposes specific design and implementation requirements on a CKMS that can be used as an FCKMS, and provides additional requirements for testing, procurement, installation, configuration, administration, operation, maintenance and use.

2.9 Example of a Distributed CKMS Supporting a Secure E-Mail Application

In the Framework, this section provides a useful example of a secure email application.

2.10 Modules, Devices, and Components

This Profile uses the term "component" to mean any hardware, software, and/or firmware required to construct a CKMS. The term "device" denotes a combination of components that function together to serve a specific purpose. An FCKMS module is a device that performs a set of key and metadata management functions for at least one FCKMS.

As shown in Figure 1, an FCKMS includes one or more computers, each with an FCKMS module that interacts with the FCKMS modules in other computers, often using a means of communication that requires cryptographic protection. An FCKMS module is the hardware and/or software that can interact with identical or compatible FCKMS modules located wherever keys and their metadata are required. Each FCKMS module is associated with a cryptographic module. A cryptographic module is the hardware and/or software that performs the actual cryptographic operations, e.g., encryption, decryption and generating a digital signature. Each FCKMS module must have access to a cryptographic module that functions as a sub-module of the FCKMS module.

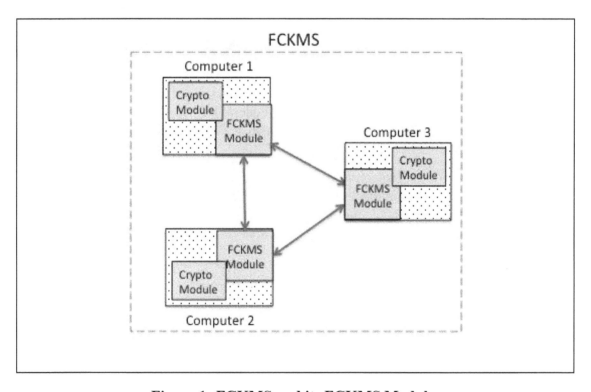

Figure 1: FCKMS and its FCKMS Modules

The cryptographic modules used in an FCKMS must be FIPS 140-validated at an appropriate FIPS 140 security level for the impact-level associated with the information that the keys will protect. A higher FIPS 140 security level than the minimum level is acceptable.

At a minimum, low impact data must be protected by employing a cryptographic module that has been validated at level 2 or higher, or at security level 1 if the FCKMS provides either identity-based or role based authentication and physical-security protection that compensates for the level 2 physical-security requirements not included in the module. Accordingly, the higher impact-levels must use cryptographic modules that provide increasingly more protection than is provided at the Low impact-level, i.e.. the Moderate impact-level requires a level 3 cryptographic module or higher, and the High impact-level requires level 4 physical security, with all other areas at security levels 3 or higher.

FR:2.5 The CKMS design **shall** specify all major devices of the CKMS (e.g., the make, model, and version).

PR:2.9	SC-13	A Federal CKMS **shall** use FIPS 140-validated cryptographic modules operating in an approved-mode of operation.
PR:2.10		Each cryptographic function used by a Federal CKMS **shall** be implemented within a FIPS-140 validated cryptographic module.
PR:2.11	SC-13	For the protection of keys and metadata used to protect data at the Low impact-level, a Federal CKMS **shall** employ cryptographic modules validated at FIPS 140 security level 2 or higher, or at security level 1 if the FCKMS provides either identity-based or role-based authentication and compensating physical security protection.
PR:2.12	SC-13	For the protection of keys and metadata used to protect data at the Moderate impact-level, a Federal CKMS **shall** employ cryptographic modules validated at FIPS 140 security level 3 or higher.
PR:2.13	SC-13	For the protection of keys and metadata used to protect data at the High impact-level, a Federal CKMS **shall** employ cryptographic modules validated at FIPS 140 physical security level 4, and all other areas at security levels 3 or higher.

PA:2.2		A Federal CKMS **should** assure that all its cryptographic modules are protected against invasive and non-invasive attacks.

3 Federal CKMS Goals

A Federal CKMS should achieve goals and satisfy requirements that are specified in the security policies of one or more Federal organizations. The typical primary security goal of an organization is to protect its information at a level commensurate with its value, sensitivity, and perceived risks. Three information-system impact-levels are defined in [FIPS 200] and [FIPS 199]: Low, Moderate, and High. As discussed in Section 8.5, Federal organizations are required to establish the appropriate impact-levels for the various categories of information processed, stored, and transmitted within Federal information systems, based on the potential adverse impact to organizational operations and assets, if such information is lost or compromised. After the impact-level is determined, the appropriate controls for an FCKMS may be selected from [SP 800-53] and this Profile (i.e., SP 800-152), and then assessed using [SP 800-53A].

3.1 Providing Key Management to Networks, Applications, and Users

The information-processing network in which an FCKMS operates is also typically used as the communications backbone of both the user's applications and the FCKMS. Network characteristics, such as error properties, could influence the selection of the cryptographic algorithms and cryptographic modes of operation, because some modes of operation extend communication errors, which could make the decrypted communication unintelligible. Other modes can minimize the effects of a communication error.

An FCKMS could provide key-management services for a single organization, application, or user, or for many of each. An FCKMS designed for a single application could be integrated into that application, while an FCKMS supporting many applications and/or users in geographically distributed locations could be distributed to wherever key-management services are needed and require communication networks to provide interaction between the distributed applications and users.

FR:3.1 The CKMS design **shall** specify its goals with respect to the communications networks on which it will function.

FR:3.2 The CKMS design **shall** specify the intended applications that it will support.

FR:3.3 The CKMS design **shall** list the intended number of users and the responsibilities that the CKMS places on those users.

3.2 Maximize the Use of COTS Products in an FCKMS

Commercial Off-The-Shelf (COTS) products that are designed and produced for many customers are typically less costly to acquire, operate, and maintain than custom products that have been designed for a single customer. A CKMS that satisfies a wide range of requirements is often a goal of CKMS designers, FCKMS service providers and FCKMS service-using organizations because of its reduced cost, wider market acceptance, and greater interoperability among FCKMSs. A COTS CKMS could be configurable to meet the special needs of multiple customers and, therefore, be widely accepted in the marketplace.

FR:3.4 The CKMS design **shall** specify the COTS products used in the CKMS.

FR:3.5 The CKMS design **shall** specify which security functions are performed by COTS products.

FR:3.6 The CKMS design **shall** specify how COTS products are configured and augmented to meet the CKMS goal.

3.3 Conformance to Standards

An FCKMS that conforms to widely accepted security standards often increases confidence in its ability to provide the desired protection, since it benefits from the wisdom that went into developing the standards. If the standards have validation programs that measure compliance and those validations are obtained, there is increased confidence that the FCKMS has implemented that standard correctly. The use of standards also fosters interoperability when different FCKMSs need to interoperate.

FR:3.7 The CKMS design **shall** specify the Federal, national, and international standards that are utilized by the CKMS.

FR:3.8 For each standard utilized by the CKMS, the CKMS design **shall** specify which CKMS devices implement the standard.

FR:3.9 For each standard utilized by the CKMS, the CKMS design **shall** specify how conformance to the standard was validated (e.g., by a third-party testing program).

PR:3.1	SC-13	A Federal CKMS **shall** specify the Federal Information Processing Standards (FIPS) and NIST Special Publications (SPs) to which the FCKMS or FCKMS devices have been validated.

PF:3.1		A Federal CKMS **could** conform to selected specifications of Industrial, National, and International standards for security and interoperability of the FCKMS.

3.4 Ease-of-use

Ease-of-use is very subjective. Something easy for one person to do may not be easy for another. An FCKMS should be easy to use by both untrained and experienced users. For example, the FCKMS could assist untrained users by performing the required actions automatically, but provide an interface for experienced users to select and use acceptable alternative actions. Negative user experiences could affect the acceptability and use of a security service or product. A Federal CKMS should be designed to support a range of user expertise and experience.

Ease-of-use testing is discussed in Section 9.8.

3.4.1 Accommodate User Ability and Preferences

An FCKMS should accommodate differences in user abilities and preferences when managing their keys and metadata. Differences generally include user knowledge, experience, task familiarity, and motivation. Preferences often vary between user control and system control.

An FCKMS could provide fully automated security services to a user or an application, based on the organizational policy. It could provide a combination of automated security services and those selected and controlled by a user or application. An FCKMS should support user control, based on organizational policy and user desires, and provide one or more security-service-control interfaces for its users and managers.

FR:3.10 The CKMS design **shall** specify all user interfaces to the system.

FR:3.11 The CKMS design **shall** specify the results of any user-acceptance tests that have been performed regarding the ease of using the proposed user interfaces.

PA:3.1		A Federal CKMS **should** support user interfaces that: a) Require minimal user interactions with the FCKMS, b) Are commensurate with the range of experience and capability of its expected users, c) Support a user initiating the generation of cryptographic keys and associated metadata, and d) Provide one or more security-service-control interfaces.

PF:3.2		A Federal CKMS **could** provide fully automated services to a user or an application, based on organizational policy.

3.4.2 Design Principles of the User Interface

Ease-of-use design goals should assure that:

a) It is intuitive and easy to do the right thing,
b) It is not easy to do the wrong thing, and
c) It is intuitive and easy to recover when a wrong thing is done.

FR:3.12 The CKMS design **shall** specify the design principles of the user interface.

FR:3.13 The CKMS design **shall** specify all human error-prevention or failsafe features designed into the system.

PR:3.2		A Federal CKMS **shall** support features that are designed to detect and/or mitigate incorrect user input.

PA:3.2		A Federal CKMS **should** support user interfaces (as needed) that assist the user in selecting and using appropriate security

		functions and services for the key-management services that they require.
PA:3.3		A Federal CKMS **should** support control interfaces (as needed) that support the Federal CKMS roles and assure that: a) It is intuitive to initiate and perform all supported key-management service-control interactions with the FCKMS (e.g., to select and invoke a key-management function); b) It is difficult to make an error or cause a security breach when initiating or interacting with an FCKMS service; and c) It is easy to recover from an FCKMS service initiation or control error.

PF:3.3		A Federal CKMS **could** support the same interfaces as used by other Federal CKMSs.

3.5 Performance and Scalability

Performance and scalability should be considered when designing a CKMS. The performance of an FCKMS will generally depend on factors that include 1) the simplicity of the overall design, 2) the number and type of service-using organizations, 3) the sensitive applications and number of users being supported, 4) the communications capabilities and geographical distribution among the distributed devices of the FCKMS, and 5) the capabilities of the computers, modules, and devices comprising it. The scalability of an FCKMS depends on such factors as the flexibility of the underlying CKMS design and implementation to support increasing service demands, and the ability to replace or upgrade its devices and components as necessary.

FR:3.14 The CKMS design **shall** specify the performance characteristics of the CKMS, including the average and peak workloads that can be handled for the types of functions and transactions implemented, and the response times for the types of functions and transactions under those respective workloads.

FR:3.15 The CKMS design **shall** specify the techniques that are supported and can be used to scale the system to increased workload demands.

FR:3.16 The CKMS design **shall** specify the extent to which the CKMS can be scaled to meet increased workload demands. This **shall** be expressed in terms of additional workload, response times for the workload, and cost.

PR:3.3		A Federal CKMS **shall** be scalable to support increasing numbers of FCKMS users and their computers, communications, and sensitive applications.

PR:3.4		A Federal CKMS-using organization **shall** identify the maximum required design capacity (e.g., the maximum number of users, the number of FKCMS computers or mobile devices, the communications bandwidth, and the applications to be supported by its FCKMS and its associated communication mechanisms).

3.6 Intellectual Property Rights

A goal of designing, implementing, and operating any system is to avoid complex and expensive litigation. Intellectual property rights, such as copyrights, trademarks, and patents should be respected as required by law. Therefore, it is best to identify and resolve possible legal issues as soon as possible.

PA:3.4		Federal CKS service-providing organizations **should** identify intellectual-property rights that apply to the design, procurement, implementation, and operation of a new or upgraded FCKMS.

4 Security Policies

An organization often creates and supports layered security policies, with high-level policies addressing the management of its information and lower-level policies specifying the rules for protecting the information.

An organization could have different policies covering different applications or categories of information. For example, a Federal organization could have one set of policies covering its financial information and a different set of policies covering its personnel information.

This section describes a layered set of policies, including an Information Management Policy, an Information Security Policy, and an FCKMS Security Policy.

4.1 Information Management Policy

An organization's Information Management Policy governs the collection, processing, and use of an organization's information, and should specify, at a high level, what information is to be collected or created, and how it is to be managed. An organization's management establishes this policy using industry standards of good practices, legal requirements regarding the organization's information, and organizational goals that must be achieved using the information that the organization will be collecting and creating.

These specifications are the foundation of an Information Security Policy (see Section 4.2) and dictate the levels of confidentiality, integrity, availability, and source-authentication protections that must be provided for each category of sensitive and valuable information covered by the Information Management Policy.

PR:4.1		A Federal CKMS service-using organization **shall** create an Information Management Policy that: a) Specifies the information to be collected or created and how it is to be managed; b) Specifies the high-level goals for obtaining and using the information; c) Specifies the organizational management roles and responsibilities for the policy and establishes the authorization required for people performing these information-management duties; d) Specifies what categories of information need to be protected against unauthorized disclosure, modification or destruction; and e) Establishes the rules for authorizing one or more people to create policy and manage its implementation and use.

4.2   Information Security Policy

An organization's Information Security Policy is created to support and enforce portions of the organization's Information Management Policy by specifying in more detail what information is to be protected from anticipated threats and how that protection is to be attained. A Federal organization may have different Information Security Policies covering different applications or categories of information (e.g., the policies may be different for non-personnel information than for personnel information).

The Information Security Policy should be used to create an FCKMS Security Policy (see Section 4.3).

| **PR:4.2** | PL-1
RA-2 | A Federal CKMS using-organization **shall** create an Information Security Policy that is consistent with the organization's Information Management Policy and specifies:

a) The categories of information that are considered sensitive;
b) The impact-level associated with the sensitive information;
c) The current, anticipated, and potential threats to the information;
d) How the necessary protection is to be obtained; and
e) The rules for collecting, protecting and distributing the sensitive information. |

4.3   CKMS and FCKMS Security Policies

This Profile is based on the assumption that a CKMS designer will either build a product that supports the specific policies of its known potential customers or one that is comprehensive and flexible enough to be configured to satisfy different security policies for a large number of future customers.

A CKMS designer creates a CKMS Security Policy to protect the cryptographic keys and metadata used by the CKMS and to enforce restrictions associated with their use. The protections should cover the entire key lifecycle, including when they are operational, stored, and transported. A CKMS Security Policy includes an identification of all cryptographic mechanisms and cryptographic protocols that can be used by the CKMS.

The FCKMS Security Policy of a security domain should be derived from the Information Management policies of all organizations comprising the security domain. All entities that constitute a security domain are responsible for being aware of and following the FCKMS Security Policy. All entities in the domain are responsible for protecting the keys and associated metadata used to cryptographically protect data in accordance with the FCKMS Security Policy.

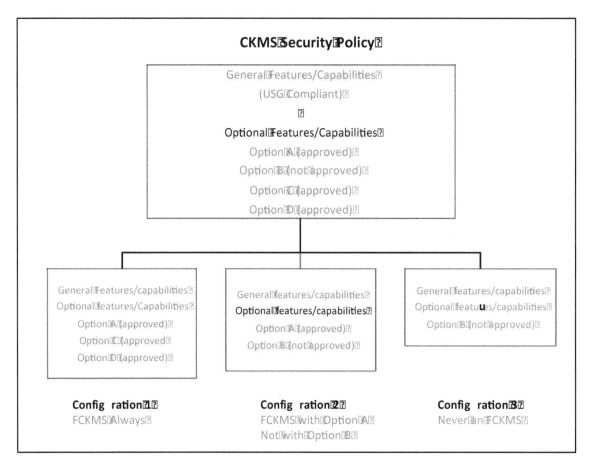

Figure 2: CKMS Security Policy Configurations

An FCKMS Security Policy is intended to support the Information Security Policy of the FCKMS service-using organization(s) by specifying the rules for managing the cryptographic keys and metadata used to protect the information. An FCKMS Security Policy may be a configured subset of the designer's CKMS Security Policy, which specifically meets Federal government requirements and also the specific requirements of the service-using organization(s). See Figure 2 for an example.

Figure 2 depicts a CKMS Security Policy (in the top-level box) with general features and capabilities, as well as optional features/capabilities that can be selected or prohibited to create a sub-policy appropriate for a specific CKMS service provider. The green text is used to indicate features that are compliant with the United States Government (USG) requirements of this document. Options A, C, and D (indicated in green text) are all approved for USG use. However, Option B (indicated by red text) is not approved. For example, Option B may involve the use of a cryptographic algorithm that is not approved for USG use. The second-level boxes show three possible configurations that could be selected using the CKMS options. Configuration 1 contains Options A, C, and D; Configuration 2 contains Options A and B; and Configuration 3 contains only Option B. Configuration 1 can always function as an FCKMS, since all its features and options are consistent with USG use. Configuration 2 can function as an FCKMS when Option A is used, but it can function only as a CKMS when Option B is used. Finally, Configuration 3 can never function as an FCKMS, since the non-approved Option B is always used. Federal agencies could always use Configuration 1. They could use Configuration 2 if only Option A was selected, but they could never use Configuration 3 for sensitive U.S. Government data.

Ultimately, it is the responsibility of the organization that owns the data to assure that the data is properly protected. That organization is often the FCKMS service-using organization. An FCKMS service-using organization must use an FCKMS that supports a security policy that is consistent with its higher-level policies (e.g., its Information Management Policy and Information Security Policy) and other applicable U.S. Government requirements. A Federal organization that is considering the procurement of a CKMS or the services of a CKMS provider should review the security policy of each candidate CKMS and verify that the CKMS has the necessary capabilities. An appropriate FCKMS Security Policy should then be created. The FCKMS Security Policy should specify the rules that can assure the availability, confidentiality, and integrity of the organization's cryptographic keys and bound metadata that will be used to protect the sensitive information to be protected by the FCKMS. An FCKMS service-using organization should verify that its security policies are consistent with, and can be supported by, an FCKMS service provider, both administratively and technically.

The FCKMS Security Policy should specify how to protect each type of key and its associated metadata throughout their lifecycles, including when they are stored, transported, or used.

An FCKMS service-using organization should assist in adopting, supporting, and enforcing its own security policies and implementation rules by providing for tutorials to new managers and users on how services should be managed and used. If a user can select and initiate security services for an application or category of information, then the FCKMS service-providing organization should assist in selecting appropriate security services by informing the user of the rules and how the rules can and should be followed. The FCKMS should be configured so as to minimize the likelihood that a user could select an inappropriate option.

FR:4.1 The CKMS design **shall** specify the CKMS Security Policy, including the configurable options and sub-policies that it is designed to enforce.

FR:4.2 The CKMS design **shall** specify how the CKMS Security Policy is to be enforced by the CKMS (e.g., the mechanisms used to provide the protection required by the policy).

FR:4.3 The CKMS design **shall** specify how any automated portions of the CKMS Security Policy are expressed in an unambiguous tabular form or a formal language (e.g., XML or ASN.1), such that an automated security system (e.g., table driven or syntax-directed software mechanisms) in the CKMS can enforce them.

PR:4.3	PL-1	A Federal CKMS **shall** have an FCKMS Security Policy that is consistent with the higher-level security policies of its service-using organization(s).
PR:4.4		A Federal CKMS **shall** support its FCKMS Security Policy.

PR:4.5	PL-1	A Federal CKMS **shall** make its FCKMS Security Policy available to all its FCKMS service-using organizations and their authorized users.
PR:4.6	AT-2	Federal CKMS users and managers **shall** receive training about the security policies relevant to the FCKMS and the use of the FCKMS in accordance with those policies.

PA:4.1		The FCKMS Security Policy **should** specify the following: a) The names of the organization(s) adopting the policy; b) Who (person, title or role) is authorized to approve/modify the policy, c) The impact-levels of the information that is specified in and controlled by the policy, d) The primary data and key/metadata protection services (i.e., data confidentiality, data integrity, source authentication) that are to be provided by the FCKMS, e) The security services (e.g., personal accountability, personal privacy, availability, anonymity, unlinkability, unobservability) that can be supported by the FCKMS, f) Sensitivity and handling restrictions for keys and associated metadata, g) The algorithms and all associated parameters to be used for each impact-level and with each protection service, h) The expected maximum lifetime of keys and metadata for each cryptographic algorithm used, i) The acceptable methods of user/role and source authentication for each information impact-level to be protected by a key and its associated metadata, j) The backup, archiving and recovery requirements for keys and metadata at each information impact-level, k) The roles to be supported by the FCKMS, l) The access control and physical security requirements for the FCKMS's keys and metadata for each impact-level, m) The means and rules for recovering keys and metadata, and n) The communication protocols to be used when protecting sensitive data, keys, and metadata.

A security policy should be written so that the people responsible for managing and using the policy can understand the goals of the policy and can follow its implementation rules. A security policy could be encoded in an electronic form (e.g., a policy specification formal language, table of security rules, or computer program) such that an FCKMS could automatically support and enforce parts of the policy. Automated security policy support systems could be programmed to detect security problems and resolve them in accordance with the policy.

A Security policy can be described in a formal language that can be used to explicitly define the syntax (i.e., acceptable sentences) of a policy such that a computer program can recognize and follow the rules of the policy. These rules could be called the semantics (i.e., acceptable meaning) of each sentence of the language. If a security policy is encoded correctly, a Federal CKMS could support and enforce it.

PF:4.1		A Federal CKMS **could** support its administrators in assessing a security policy for completeness and enforceability.

4.4 FCKMS Module Security Policy

As shown in Figure 1 of Section 2.10, an FCKMS consists of one or more computers containing an FCKMS module, with an associated cryptographic module. The computer could, in fact, have more than one FCKMS module and more than one cryptographic module. Each FCKMS module is designed to support one or more FCKMSs, along with their FCKMS Security Policies.

Each FCKMS module must have its own FCKMS Module Security Policy, which supports one or more FCKMS Security Policies. However, the security policy for an FCKMS module may not be a full FCKMS Security Policy. The FCKMS Module Security Policy need only deal with the subset of the FCKMS Security Policy that applies to the module itself.

Figure 3 depicts an example of a network consisting of three Federal Entities and three FCKMSs, each with its own FCKMS Security Policy as indicated by the colors red, blue, and green. The arrowed lines between FCKMS modules indicate communications links over which cryptographic keys and metadata may be established according to the policy indicated by the color of the line. Thus, Federal Entity 1 can establish keys with Federal Entity 2 using the blue FCKMS with the blue FCKMS Security Policy. Federal Entity 1 can also establish keys with Federal Entity 3 using the red FCKMS with the red FCKMS Security Policy. Finally, Federal Entity 1 could store keys that it uses only for its own purposes using the green FCKMS with the green FCKMS Security Policy.

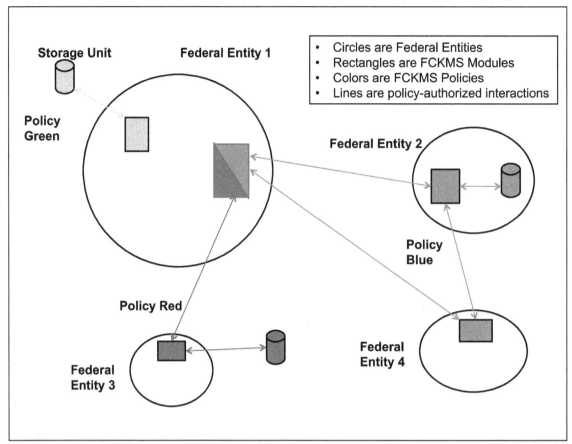

Figure 3: An FCKMS Network

Figure 3 shows that a module may function in different FCKMSs and support different
FCKMS Security Policies. For example, Federal Entity 1 has a module that can support
either a blue FCKMS Security Policy or a red FCKMS Security Policy. Such FCKMS
modules must be capable of maintaining the separation of the keys and metadata of each
FCKMS that it supports. Federal Entity 3 cannot exchange keys and metadata with Federal
Entity 2 or Federal Entity 4 unless the red and blue FCKMS Security Policies are determined
to be equivalent or compatible (see Section 4.11.3) by the red and blue system authorities.

PR:4.7	PL-1	An FCKMS module **shall** have an FCKMS Module Security Policy that identifies the subsets of all known FCKMS Security Policies that it supports.
PR:4.8	AC-4 (22)	An FCKMS module that interacts with multiple non-equivalent and non-compatible FCKMSs **shall** support the separation of keys and metadata of each FCKMS from each other FCKMS.

4.5 Cryptographic Module Security Policy

A cryptographic module security policy is a statement of the rules that the cryptographic
module will follow when performing cryptographic functions (e.g., key generation and
signature verification). This policy specifies the mechanisms to be used to maintain the

security of the module and to protect sensitive data, including secret and private plaintext keys and sensitive metadata. The cryptographic module security policy includes specifications for controlling access to the keys and metadata, the physical security provided to protect the module's storage and processing capabilities, and the mitigation of other attacks specified in the policy. See [FIPS 140] for further information.

4.6   Other Related Security Policies

An FCKMS Security Policy could include or rely on other security policies or provisions, such as a Physical Security Policy, a Communications Security Policy, and/or a Computer Security Policy. Organizations typically develop their own physical security policies, and computer systems are often built to their own computer security policies. An organization should organize these policies in a logical structure that assigns roles for managing and enforcing the policies to appropriate parts of the organization.

FR:4.4 The CKMS design **shall** specify other related security policies that support the CKMS Security Policy.

PA:4.2		Federal CKMS service-using organizations **should** coordinate with their service-providing organization in defining and supporting security policies for providing key-management services for their users.
PA:4.3		A Federal CKMS service provider **should** have a Computer Security Policy.
PA:4.4		A Federal CKMS service-using organization **should** create a Computer Security Policy that identifies: a) The information that is processed, communicated, and stored within its computer systems that requires protection, b) The threats that are to be protected against, and c) The detailed rules for protecting the information by computers, communication systems, and computer users.
PA:4.5		A Federal CKMS **should** use and support applications using computer operating systems that provide security in accordance with the FCKMS service-using organization's Computer Security Policy.

4.7   Interrelationships among Policies

The Information Management Policy, Information Security Policy, FCKMS Security Policy, FCKMS Module Security Policy, Cryptographic Module Security Policy and other related security policies typically form a top-down layered set of policies in which a lower-layer policy supports the policy/policies at the higher layers. For example, an Information Management Policy for protecting certain categories of information from unauthorized disclosure may result in an Information Security Policy for encrypting data before being transmitted or stored. This Policy may dictate an FCKMS Security Policy specifying the use of symmetric-key encryption/decryption using a specific algorithm and key length. The FCKMS Module Security Policy may specify the necessary key and metadata management functions, and the Cryptographic Module Security Policy would describe how the keys would be protected while in a Cryptographic Module.

FR:4.5 The CKMS design **shall** specify the policies that are supported by the CKMS design and a summary of how they are supported by the design.

PR:4.9	PL-1	A Federal CKMS **shall** document the relationships among its policies.
PR:4.10		The security policies of a Federal CKMS **shall** be compatible with each other.

4.8   Personal Accountability

A Personal Accountability Policy requires that every person who accesses sensitive information be held accountable for his or her actions. Personal accountability may be a requirement in an Information Management Policy that needs to be supported by specific features in the FCKMS for the management of keys and metadata, such as an access control system that requires users to authenticate their identity before access is granted to an FCKMS capability.

An FCKMS that supports a Personal Accountability Policy needs to be able to correctly identify each person accessing and using the FCKMS, determine who is authorized to access controlled items, grant access only upon verification of the authorization, and detect and report any attempts for unauthorized access.

FR:4.6 The CKMS design **shall** specify if and how personal accountability is supported by the CKMS.

PR:4.11		A Federal CKMS operating at the Moderate or High impact-level **shall** provide personal accountability for all entities acting in all roles provided by the Federal CKMS.

PR:4.12	AC-2 AC-3 IA-2	In order to provide personal accountability, a Federal CKMS operating at the Moderate or High impact-level **shall**: a) Perform identity-based authentication (e.g., of users), b) Verify entity access authorization, c) Detect requests for unauthorized access, d) Report requests for unauthorized access to the audit administrator, e) Restrict the use of an FCKMS to authorized entities performing authorized activities, and f) Detect attempts to bypass personal accountability policy and report each such offense to FCKMS management.

PA:4.6		A Federal CKMS operating at the Low impact-level **should** provide personal accountability for all entities acting in all roles provided by the Federal CKMS.
PA:4.7		In order to provide personal accountability, a Federal CKMS operating at the Low impact-level **should**: a) Perform identity-based authentication (e.g., of devices and users), b) Verify entity access authorization, c) Detect requests for unauthorized access, d) Report requests for unauthorized access to the audit administrator, e) Restrict the use of an FCKMS to authorized entities performing authorized activities, and f) Detect attempts to bypass personal accountability policy and report each such offense to FCKMS management.

4.9 Anonymity, Unlinkability, and Unobservability

An Information Security Policy could require that certain users or categories of users of a secure information-processing system be assured of anonymity, unlinkability, and/or unobservability.

a) Anonymity assures that an entity cannot be associated with specific information or actions;

b) Unlinkability assures that two or more events in an information processing system cannot be determined to be related; and

   c) Unobservability assures that an attacker is unable to identify or infer the existence of a transaction and the identities of the entities that initiate or participate in the transaction.

FR:4.7 The CKMS design **shall** specify the anonymity, unlinkability, and unobservability policies that can be supported by the CKMS.

4.9.1 Anonymity

An FCKMS often requires information about the identity of entities participating in FCKMS transactions (e.g., to determine the keys to be used); an entity assuming the audit role may also require this information. However, an FCKMS could protect the anonymity of the entities operating in the user role when viewed by entities assuming non-audit roles and entities not involved in the transactions. Since personal accountability is required at the Moderate and High impact-levels, anonymity can only be provided at the Low impact-level.

FR:4.8 The CKMS design **shall** specify which CKMS transactions have or can be provided with anonymity protection.

FR:4.9 The CKMS design **shall** specify how CKMS transaction anonymity is achieved when anonymity assurance is provided.

PR:4.13		A Federal CKMS **shall not** provide anonymity for Moderate or High impact-level data.
PR:4.14		When anonymity is provided, a Federal CKMS **shall** assure that a key owner's true identity cannot be determined when viewed by entities assuming non-audit roles and entities not involved in the transactions.

4.9.2 Unlinkability

An FCKMS may need to link FCKMS transactions together, e.g., a transaction that requests the generation of a key, and another that uses it; an entity assuming the audit role may also require this information. However, an FCKMS could provide unlinkability protection of FCKMS transactions such that entities cannot be linked to initiating or participating in an FCKMS transaction when viewed from outside the FCKMS or by entities assuming non-audit roles within the FCKMS that are not involved in those transactions.

FR:4.10 The CKMS design **shall** specify which CKMS transactions have or can be provided with unlinkability protection.

FR:4.11 The CKMS design **shall** specify how CKMS transaction unlinkability is achieved.

PR:4.15		When unlinkability is required, a Federal CKMS **shall** assure that unauthorized entities within the system cannot link two or more transactions with each other or with the participants in the transactions.

4.9.3 Unobservability

An FCKMS could protect the existence of transactions and the identities of the entities that initiate or participate in the transactions from being observed (i.e., monitored, recorded).

FR:4.12 The CKMS design **shall** specify which CKMS transactions have or can be provided with unobservability protection.

FR:4.13 The CKMS design **shall** specify how CKMS transaction unobservability is achieved.

PR:4.16		When unobservability is required, a Federal CKMS **shall** assure that any key-management transaction is not observable by anyone except authorized entities.

4.10 Laws, Rules, and Regulations

The security policies of an organization should conform to the laws, rules, and regulations of the locality, state, and nation(s) in which its FCKMS will be used. If an FCKMS is designed for international use, then it should be flexible enough to conform to the restrictions of multiple nations.

FR:4.14 The CKMS design **shall** specify the countries and/or regions of countries where it is intended for use and any legal restrictions that the CKMS is intended to enforce.

PR:4.17	SC-1	A Federal CKMS **shall** comply with U.S. Federal laws, rules and regulations.

PA:4.8		A Federal CKMS **should** comply with the rules and regulations of the countries in which it is operating and providing key-management services.

PF:4.2		A Federal CKMS **could be** configurable to comply with the policies of one or more national and international organizations.

4.11 Security Domains

A security domain is a collection of entities that support the same FCKMS Security Policy (see Section 4.3). When two mutually trusting entities are operating in the same security domain, the entities can exchange keys and metadata while providing the protections that are required by the FCKMS Security Policy.

Security domains can be useful when managing an organization's users and computers that can connect to users and computers in other organizations. If different entities are in the same Security Domain, sharing information securely is relatively easy. If they are in different Security Domains, then the sharing of information becomes difficult or even impossible.

When two entities are in different security domains, they may not be able to provide equivalent protection to the exchanged keys and metadata because they are operating in different FCKMSs under different FCKMS Security Policies. However, there are circumstances in which an entity in one domain can send keys and metadata to another entity in a different domain, even though their policies are not identical.

Before information is shared between entities in two or more Security Domains, their FCKMS Security Policies must be carefully examined before exchanging or combining their information. The domain authorities for the domains intending to share information should verify that the different FCKMS Security Policies provide acceptable protection for each other's data. Computers could verify the equivalence or compatibility of two or more FCKMS Security Policies if they are encoded to enable such verification.

A security domain could be defined for a single information impact-level (e.g., Low) or could be defined for multiple impact-levels (e.g., Low and Moderate). The computer systems that are processing multiple levels of sensitive information must be designed, programmed, and operated to separate and protect the processing of information at the different impact-levels.

4.11.1 Conditions for Data Exchange

Both the entity intending to send sensitive data to another entity in a different domain, and the intended receiving entity, should satisfy the following conditions:

 a) Have an acceptable means of sending and receiving the information (i.e., the communications channel with agreed-upon protocols),

 b) Have interoperable cryptographic capabilities (e.g., identical encryption/decryption algorithms that utilize identical key lengths),

 c) Have acceptable FCKMS Security Policies for exchanging information, and

 d) Trust each other to enforce their FCKMS Security Policies.

If two entities belong to the same security domain, it is likely that these conditions can be met. If the entities do not belong to the same security domain, then these conditions are less likely to be satisfied. See Section 4.9.2 of the Framework for additional information.

FR:4.15 The CKMS design **shall** specify design features that allow for the exchange of keys and metadata with entities in other security domains that are considered to offer equivalent but different security protections.

4.11.2 Assurance of Protection

Protection assurances within security domains include protecting a key and/or metadata from unauthorized disclosure and unauthorized modification, as well as verifying the source and destination of a key and/or metadata.

FR:4.16 The CKMS design **shall** specify the source and destination authentication policies that it enforces when sharing a key and/or metadata with entities in differing security domains.

FR:4.17 The CKMS design **shall** specify the confidentiality and integrity policies that it enforces when sharing a key and/or metadata with entities in differing security domains.

FR:4.18 The CKMS design **shall** specify what assurances it requires when communicating with entities from other security domains.

4.11.3 Equivalence and Compatibility of FCKMS Security Policies

When entities in different security domains need to share or mix data, their respective security policies must be equivalent or compatible.

Two security domains have equivalent FCKMS Security Policies if the authority responsible for each security domain agrees to accept the other domain's FCKMS Security Policy as being equivalent to its own FCKMS Security Policy in terms of the security protections, including the levels of protection provided. If it is determined that the policies of two FCKMSs are equivalent, then an entity in one security domain may share data with an entity in another equivalent domain.

Two security domains are compatible if they can exchange a key and its metadata without changing the protection provided to the key and metadata and without violating (or altering) either domain's FCKMS Security Policy. For example, suppose that domain 1 allows domain 1 entities to bind keys and metadata using RSA-2048, and domain 2 allows domain 2 entities to receive and verify the binding on keys with RSA-2048, but domain 1 does not permit using RSA-2048 for verifying the binding on keys, and domain 2 does not permit using RSA-2048 for binding keys. Clearly, their security policies are different and not equivalent, yet a key may be sent from a domain 1 entity to a domain 2 entity because the two domains are compatible for a transaction that sends a key from domain 1 to domain 2.

FR:4.19 The CKMS design **shall** specify if and how it supports the review and verification of another domain's security before intra-domain communications are permitted.

FR:4.20 The CKMS design **shall** specify how it detects, prevents or warns an entity of the possible security consequences of communicating with an entity in a security domain with weaker policies.

PF:4.3		A Federal CKMS **could** support the authorities from different security domains in reviewing each other's FCKMS Security Policies and verifying their equivalence or compatibility.
PF:4.4	AC-4 (20)	A Federal CKMS **could** support key-management services for the sharing of sensitive data among two or more domains whose FCKMS security policies have been verified as being equivalent or compatible.

PF:4.5	AC-4 (20)	A Federal CKMS **could** support protocols that obtain an FCKMS Security Policy from a different security domain, compare the obtained policy to the local FCKMS Security Policy, and establish whether the obtained policy is equivalent to or compatible with the local FCKMS Security Policy.
PF:4.6		The domain authorities of Federal CKMSs **could** negotiate and institute a common FCKMS Security Policy for protecting the data of both domains using the following actions: a) Agree on the common FCKMS Security Policy, b) Notify all entities of the planned FCKMS Security Policy change, and c) Verify that each domain enforces the common FCKMS Security Policy.

4.11.4 Third-Party Sharing

When two domain authorities examine each other's FCKMS Security Policy for equivalence to or compatibility with their own FCKMS Security Policy, they should carefully examine each other's policies for sharing keys, metadata and other information with other third-party entities. For example, if domain A shares keys with domain B, can domain B share the same key and metadata with an equivalent domain C? See the Framework for further discussion.

4.11.5 Multi-level Security Domains

A security domain could contain information having more than one impact-level (e.g., Moderate and High). In this case, an FCKMS must support key management for protecting the information at both impact-levels. For this multi-level situation, the security domain acts much like two separate security domains because it must distinguish between the two levels of protection. Each entity in the domain must ensure 1) that keys and/or metadata protected by the higher-level policy are always provided with the higher level of protection, 2) that keys and/or metadata protected by the lower-level policy cannot be confused with the higher-level keys and/or metadata, and 3) that higher-level keys and/or metadata do not get confused with lower-level keys and/or metadata. This typically involves a multi-level secure computer operating system.

FR:4.21 The CKMS design **shall** specify whether or not it supports multi-level security domains.

FR:4.22 The CKMS design **shall** specify each level of security domain that it supports.

FR:4.23 If multi-level security domains are supported, the CKMS design **shall** specify how it maintains the separation of the keys and metadata belonging to each security level.

PF:4.7	AC-4 (20)	A multi-level Federal CKMS **could** support a transaction between an entity from one security domain and an entity from another security domain by: a) Determining if the two FCKMS Security Policies are multi-level, b) Determining if the two policies have an acceptable intersection of the level of protection that can be provided for the information to be exchanged, and c) Supporting that level of protection.
PF:4.8		A Federal CKMS **could** support one or more multi-level security domains.

4.11.6 Upgrading and Downgrading

Under certain conditions, a domain authority could decide that a key and/or metadata from an entity in a lower-level security domain (a domain providing less protection) can be accepted and protected at the higher level required by its own FCKMS Security Policy. This process is called upgrading. Upgrading should only be done if the authority responsible for the higher-level domain trusts the source and authenticity of the key and/or metadata to be provided from the lower level. Likewise, the domain authority for a higher-level security domain might need to pass a key and/or metadata to a lower-level security domain entity, requiring the protection on the key and/or metadata to be downgraded. In this case, the domain authority for the higher-level domain must be assured that the key and/or metadata being passed down only require the lower level of security provided by the receiver's lower-level domain.

FR:4.24 The CKMS design **shall** specify if and how it supports the upgrading or downgrading of keys and metadata.

FR:4.25 The CKMS design **shall** specify how upgrading or downgrading capabilities are restricted to the domain authority.

PR:4.18		In a Federal CKMS, upgrading and downgrading **shall** be under the control of an authorized domain authority.
PR:4.19		In a Federal CKMS, a key and its associated metadata **shall** only be upgraded if the authority responsible for the higher-level domain trusts the source and authenticity of the key and/or metadata to be provided from the lower level domain.
PR:4.20		In a Federal CKMS, a key and its associated metadata **shall** only be downgraded if the domain authority for the higher-level domain has determined that the key and/or metadata being passed down only requires the lower level of security provided by the lower-level domain.

4.11.7 Changing FCKMS Security Policies

It may be desirable to change an FCKMS Security Policy. Some FCKMSs could have been designed so that their FCKMS Security Policies can be configured to permit changes. The domain authority should approve any policy change before it is made. It is the responsibility of the Domain Authority initiating the change to inform other affected Security Domain Authorities (e.g., other domains that have been determined to be equivalent or compatible) when such changes to a security policy are made.

FR:4.26 The CKMS design **shall** specify if and how its key and/or metadata management functions may be configured to support differing FCKMS Security Policies and differing applications.

FR:4.27 The CKMS design **shall** specify if and how it can support changes in its FCKMS Security Policy by being reconfigured to accommodate communications with entities in different security domains.

PR:4.21	SA-11	A Federal CKMS **shall** perform the following actions before a changed FCKMS Security Policy is put into effect: a) Document the new FCKMS Security Policy; b) Evaluate its potential security consequences; c) Approve the changes for the modified security domain; d) Approve and implement the required FCKMS modifications, validate their correct implementation, and then test the modified FCKMS; e) Verify the correct and secure operation of the changed security-domain protection mechanisms; and f) Coordinate with the domain authorities of other domains with which an equivalence or compatibility has previously been determined.

PF:4.9		A Federal CKMS **could** support the manual configuration and/or automated negotiation of modified FCKMS Security Policies for interaction with entities in different domains that are approved by all affected Security Domain authorities.

5   Roles and Responsibilities

An FCKMS could interface with humans who are performing specific management, user, and/or operator roles. Each role should have specific requirements for a person that will be authorized to perform it.   Each person that is authorized to perform a role should be provided access to a set of key and metadata management functions that will assist in carrying out the responsibilities of the role. In order to be authorized to perform a role and its associated functions, each entity must be authenticated; note that this is a requirement for all FCKMS impact-levels. This requirement may be satisfied by identity-based authentication at all impact-levels or role-based authentication at the Low impact-level. Also, note that role-based authentication is a less restrictive requirement than personal accountability, which is addressed in Section 4.8.

Examples of FCKMS roles include, but are not limited to, the following. A description of each role is provided in the Framework.

a) System Authority,

b) System Administrator,

c) Cryptographic Officer,

d) Domain Authority,

e) Key Custodian,

f) Key Owner,

g) CKMS User,

h) Audit Administrator,

i) Registration Agent,

j) Key-Recovery Agent, and

k) CKMS Operator.

Multiple individuals could be assigned to perform a role, and/or one person could be authorized to perform multiple roles. The same individual should not perform certain roles indefinitely. It is prudent to periodically (and perhaps randomly) rotate individuals among different roles to minimize the likelihood of long-term abuses. All persons should be properly trained for the roles that they are assigned to perform. Highly sensitive roles may require multiple individuals to perform the role (e.g., multiparty control).

FR:5.1 The CKMS design **shall** specify each role employed by the CKMS, the responsibilities of each role, and how entities are assigned to each role.

FR:5.2 The CKMS design **shall** specify the key and metadata management functions (see Section 6.4) that can be used by entities fulfilling each role employed by the CKMS.

FR:5.3 The CKMS design **shall** specify which roles require role separation.

FR:5.4 The CKMS design **shall** specify how the role separation is maintained for the roles that require role separation.

FR:5.5 The CKMS design **shall** specify all automated provisions for identifying security violations, whether by individuals performing authorized roles (insiders) or by those with no authorized role (outsiders).

PR:5.1	AC-2	A Federal CKMS **shall** support the roles of System Authority, System Administrator, Audit Administrator, Cryptographic Officer and User, in addition to other roles specified in its CKMS design.
PR:5.2	AT-3	Federal CKMS personnel **shall** be trained to perform their respective roles and to maintain security.
PR:5.3	AC-2 AC-3 AC-5 AC-6 AC-24	A Federal CKMS **shall** verify the authorization of the entity initiating one or more activities while performing a role, and restrict the activities of the person performing the role to those allowed by the specification of the role.
PR:5.4		In order to verify the authorization of the entity initiating one or more activities while performing a role, a Federal CKMS supporting Moderate or High impact-level systems **shall** support identity-based authentication.
PR:5.5		In order to verify the authorization of the entity initiating one or more activities while performing a role, a Federal CKMS supporting Low impact-level systems **shall** support either identity-based authentication or role-based authentication.
PR:5.6	AC-5	A Federal CKMS **shall** ensure that a person fulfilling the role of Audit Administrator cannot fulfill additional roles other than the user role.

PA:5.1		A Federal CKMS **should** support the roles of Key Custodian, and Key Owner.
PA:5.2		Other than the user role, the roles assumed in a Federal CKMS **should** be rotated periodically.

PF:5.1		A Federal CKMS **could** support the roles of Domain Authority, Registration Agent, Key-Recovery Agent, and FCKMS Operator.

6 Cryptographic Algorithms, Keys, and Metadata

6.1 Cryptographic Algorithms and Keys

Cryptographic algorithms and their keys can be categorized according to their properties and uses. Algorithms and keys can be categorized as being symmetric (with secret keys) or asymmetric (with key pairs, one being public and the other private). Keys can be static (i.e., long term) or ephemeral (i.e., typically used only for a single secure session or key management transaction). Cryptographic algorithms can be used for signature generation, signature verification, data integrity, entity identity verification, information encryption and decryption, and random number generation (RNG). Each type of cryptographic algorithm requires a type of key appropriate for that algorithm and its current application. Key uses include signature, authentication, encryption/decryption, key wrapping, random number generation (RNG), master key, key transport, key agreement, and authorization. General requirements relating to cryptographic algorithms and key strengths have been addressed in Section 2.1.

6.1.1 Key Types, Lengths and Strengths

The Framework provides a list of twenty-one key types (shown below in Table 1) and a short description of each key type.

Table 1: Key Types

Key Type
1) Private Signature Key
2) Public Signature Key
3) Symmetric Authentication Key
4) Private Authentication Key
5) Public Authentication Key
6) Symmetric Data Encryption/Decryption Key
7) Symmetric Key Wrapping Key
8) Symmetric RNG Key
9) Private RNG Key
10) Public RNG Key
11) Symmetric Master Key
12) Private Key Transport Key
13) Public Key Transport Key
14) Symmetric Key Agreement Key
15) Private Static Key Agreement Key
16) Public Static Key Agreement Key
17) Private Ephemeral Key Agreement Key
18) Public Ephemeral Key Agreement Key
19) Symmetric Authorization Key
20) Private Authorization Key
21) Public Authorization Key

FR:6.1 The CKMS design **shall** specify and define each key type used.

PR:6.1		A Federal CKMS **shall** support all the key types and lengths required by its FCKMS Security Policy.

6.1.2 Key Protections

All keys managed by an FCKMS require integrity protection. Secret and private keys also require confidentiality protection. FIPS-validated cryptographic modules have been designed to provide this protection when used in accordance with the associated security policy. However, when outside a FIPS-validated cryptographic module, either physical or logical protection is required for these keys. Cryptographic protection is one form of logical protection.

PR:6.2	SC-8 SC-11 SC-12 SC-28	A Federal CKMS **shall** physically or logically protect all cryptographic keys from unauthorized disclosure, use, and modification.
PR:6.3		A Federal CKMS **shall** support the protection of keys at the same or a higher impact-level than the data to be protected by the keys.
PR:6.4	SC-8 SC-11 SC-12 SC-28	A Federal CKMS used to protect Moderate or High impact-level information **shall** cryptographically protect all keys against unauthorized disclosure and modification when outside a cryptographic module.

PA:6.1	SC-8 SC-11 SC-12 SC-28	A Federal CKMS used to protect Low impact-level information **should** cryptographically protect all keys against unauthorized disclosure and modification when outside a cryptographic module.

6.1.3 Key Assurance

When cryptographic keys and domain parameters[4] are stored or distributed, they may pass through unprotected environments. In this case, specific assurances are required before the key and/or domain parameters may be used to perform cryptographic operations. Assurance of integrity is needed for all keys and metadata. Assurance of possession is needed for both secret and private keys. Assurance of domain parameter validity is needed for certain public-key algorithms. Assurance of validity is needed for symmetric keys and the key pairs of public-key algorithms (which includes pairwise consistency). See [SP 800-89], [SP 800-56A] and [SP 800-56B] for further discussion. Other assurances that may be needed include source authenticity.

---

[4] Note that domain parameters used in conjunction with some public-key algorithms to generate key pairs, to create digital signatures, or to establish keying material, should not be confused with security domains.

PR:6.5	SI-7	A Federal CKMS **shall** apply integrity protection to all keys before transmission and/or storage, and verify the integrity of all keys when received or before initial use.
PR:6.6	SI-10	A Federal CKMS **shall** obtain the following assurances (as appropriate) before the initial operational use of a key: a) Domain parameter validity, b) Key pair validity, c) Private-key possession, and/or d) Secret-key possession and validity.
PR:6.7		A Federal CKMS **shall** obtain all key and domain parameter assurances using NIST-approved methods.
PR:6.8		For Moderate and High impact-level systems, a Federal CKMS **shall** support assuring a receiver of a transported key that it came from an authenticated and authorized source.

PA:6.2		For Low impact-level systems, a Federal CKMS **should** support assuring a receiver of a transported key that it came from an authenticated and authorized source.

6.2 Key Metadata

Key metadata is defined as information associated with a particular key that is managed by the FCKMS.

The CKMS designer should select the metadata that is appropriate for a trusted association with a key, based upon a number of factors, including the key type, the key lifecycle states, and the CKMS Security Policy.

6.2.1 Metadata Elements

The following are metadata elements that are described in the Framework and may be explicitly recorded. The descriptions in the Framework should be carefully reviewed when making decisions with regard to their applicability. The metadata elements are:

a) Key label,
b) Key identifier,
c) Owner identifier,
d) Key lifecycle state,
e) Key format specifier,
f) Product used to create the key,
g) Cryptographic algorithm using the key,
h) Schemes or modes of operation,
i) Parameters for the key,
j) Length of the key,
k) Security strength of the key/algorithm pair,

l) Key type,

m) Appropriate application(s) for the key,

n) Key security policy identifier,

o) Key list (ACL),

p) Key usage count,

q) Parent key: This element could have two sub-elements:
    i. Key identifier, and
    ii. Nature of the relationship.

r) Key sensitivity,

s) Key protections: This element could have several sub-elements:
    i.   The mechanism used for integrity protection,
    ii. The mechanism used for confidentiality protection
    iii. The mechanism used for source authentication, and
    iv. An indication of the protections that are enforced by a particular non-cryptographic trusted process.

t) Metadata protections: This element could have several sub-elements:
    i.   The mechanism used for integrity protection,
    ii. The mechanism used for confidentiality protection,
    iii. The mechanism used for source authentication, and
    iv. An indication of the protections that are enforced by a particular non-cryptographic trusted process.

u) Trusted association protections: The following may need to be provided for each trusted association protection:
    i. The mechanism used for integrity protection, and
    ii. The mechanism used for source authentication.

v) Date-Times:
    i.   The generation date,
    ii.   The association date,
    iii. The activation date,
    iv.   The future activation date,
    v.   The renewal date,
    vi.   The future renewal data,
    vii. The date of the last rekey,
    viii. The future rekey date,
    ix.   The date of the last usage of the key,
    x.   The deactivation date,
    xi.   The future deactivation date,
    xii. The expiration date,
    xiii. The revocation date,
    xiv. The compromise date,
    xv.   The destruction date, and
    xvi. The future destruction date.

w) Revocation Reason.

These metadata elements specify a key's important characteristics, its acceptable uses, and other information that is related to the key. This information is used by an FCKMS when managing and protecting the key. Metadata elements relevant to the management and use of a key should be correctly associated with a key and used whenever a key is stored, retrieved, loaded into a cryptographic module, used to protect data (e.g., other keys), exchanged with peer entities authorized to use the key, and when assuring that a key is correctly protected.

FR:6.2 For each key type used in the system, the CKMS design **shall** specify all metadata elements selected for a trusted association, the circumstances under which the metadata elements are created and associated with the key, and the method of association (i.e., cryptographic mechanism or trusted process).

FR:6.3 For each cryptographic mechanism used in the Key Protections metadata element (item s above), the CKMS design **shall** specify the following:

i. The cryptographic algorithm: See item g) above.
ii. The parameters for the key: See item i) above.
iii. The key identifier: See item b) above.
iv. The protection value: This element contains the protection value for integrity protection, confidentiality protection, or source authentication. For example, a properly implemented MAC or digital signature technique may provide for integrity protection and/or source authentication.
v. When the protection was applied.
vi. When the protection was verified.

FR:6.4 For each non-cryptographic trusted process used in the Key Protections metadata element (item s above), the CKMS design **shall** specify the following:

i. The identifier of the process used to distinguish it from other processes, and
ii. A description of the process or a pointer to a description of the process.

FR:6.5 For each cryptographic mechanism used in the Metadata Protections metadata element (item t above), the CKMS design **shall** specify the following:

i. The cryptographic algorithm.
ii. The parameters for the key.
iii. The key identifier.
iv. The protection value (e.g., MAC, digital signature).
v. When the protection was applied.
vi. When the protection was verified.

Generally, the same mechanism will be used for the key and bound metadata, especially if the key and metadata are bundled together.

FR:6.6 For each non-cryptographic trusted process used in the Metadata Protections metadata element (item t above), the CKMS design **shall** specify the following:

i. The identifier that is used to distinguish this process from other processes, and
ii. A description of the process or a pointer to a description of the process.

FR:6.7 For each cryptographic mechanism used in the Trusted Association Protections metadata element (item u above), the CKMS design **shall** specify the following:

    i.   The cryptographic algorithm,
    ii. The parameters for the key,
    iii. The key identifier,
    iv. The protection value (e.g., MAC, digital signature),
    v. When the protection was applied, and
    vi. When the protection was verified.

FR:6.8 For each non-cryptographic trusted process used in the Trusted Association Protections metadata element (item u above), the CKMS design **shall** specify the following:

    i.   The identifier that is used to distinguish this process from other processes, and
    ii. A description of the process or a pointer to a description of the process.

FR:6.9 The CKMS design **shall** specify the accuracy and precision required for dates and times used by the system.

FR:6.10 The CKMS design **shall** specify what authoritative time sources are used to achieve the required accuracy.

FR:6.11 The CKMS design **shall** specify how authoritative time sources are used to achieve the required accuracy.

FR:6.12 The CKMS design **shall** specify which dates, times, and functions require a trusted third-party time stamp.

PR:6.9		A Federal CKMS **shall** support all metadata elements that are required to support its FCKMS Security Policy.
PR:6.10		A Federal CKMS **shall** specify which metadata elements are sensitive.
PR:6.11	SC-8 SC-11 SC-12 SC-28	A Federal CKMS **shall** physically or logically protect all sensitive metadata from unauthorized disclosure, use, and modification.
PR:6.12		A Federal CKMS **shall** support the protection of sensitive metadata at the same or a higher impact-level than the impact-level of the data to be protected by the associated key.
PR:6.13	SI-7	A Federal CKMS **shall** apply integrity protection to all metadata before transmission and storage, and verify the integrity of all metadata when received or before the initial use of the metadata.
PR:6.14		A Federal CKMS **shall** maintain the association between a key and its metadata.

PR:6.15	SC-8 SC-11 SC-12 SC-28	A Federal CKMS that protects Moderate or High impact-level information **shall** cryptographically protect sensitive metadata from unauthorized disclosure and modification when outside of a cryptographic module.
PR:6.16		A Federal CKMS **shall** use the NIST time source when access to a time source is required.
PR:6.17		A Federal CKMS that protects Moderate or High impact-level information **shall** support source authentication of the metadata elements for all cryptographic keys.

PA:6.3		A Federal CKMS **should** explicitly support one or more of the following list of metadata elements: key label, key identifiers, key owner identifier(s), and the cryptographic algorithm using the key.
PA:6.4		A Federal CKMS that protects Low impact-level information **should** cryptographically protect sensitive metadata elements against unauthorized disclosure and modification when outside a cryptographic module.
PA:6.5		A Federal CKMS that protects Low impact-level information **should** provide source authentication of the metadata elements for all cryptographic keys.

6.2.2 Required Key and Metadata Information

Each key type requires certain metadata information to be available when a key is used, whether the information is explicitly recorded as metadata or is otherwise known by the FCKMS.

FR:6.13 For each key type, the CKMS design **shall** specify the following information regarding keys and metadata elements:

a) The key type.
b) The crypto period (for static keys).
c) The method of generation.
   i. The RNG used.
   ii. A key generation specification (e.g., [FIPS 186] for signature keys, [SP 800-56A] for Diffie-Hellman key establishment keys).
d) For each metadata element, include
   i. The source of the metadata, and
   ii. How the metadata is vetted,
e) The method of key establishment
   i. The key transport scheme (if used),
   ii. The key agreement scheme (if used), and
   iii. The protocol name (if a named protocol is used).
f) The disclosure protections (e.g., key confidentiality, physical security).

g) The modification protections (e.g., a MAC or a digital signature).
h) The applications that may use the key (e.g., TLS, EFS, S/MIME, IPSec, PKINIT, SSH, etc.).
i) The applications that are not permitted to use the key.
j) The key assurances:

   i. Symmetric-key assurances (e.g., format checks):
- Who obtains the assurance,
- The circumstances under which it is obtained, and
- How the assurance is obtained.

   ii. Asymmetric-key assurances (e.g., assurance of possession and validity):
- Who obtains the assurances,
- The circumstances under which the assurance is obtained, and
- How the assurance is obtained.

   iii. Domain parameter validity checks:
- Who performs the validity check,
- The circumstances under which the checking is performed, and
- How the assurance of domain parameter validity was obtained.

FR:6.14 The CKMS design **shall** specify all syntax, semantics, and formats of all key types and their metadata that will be created, stored, transmitted, processed, and otherwise managed by the CKMS.

6.3 Key Lifecycle States and Transitions

A key may pass through several states between its generation and its destruction. For a discussion of key states, see Section 7 of [SP 800-57 Part 1]. A CKMS designer will select and define the key states and transitions that will be supported by the FCKMS.

FR:6.15 The CKMS design **shall** specify all the states that the CKMS keys can attain.

FR:6.16 The CKMS design **shall** specify all transitions between the CKMS key states and the data (inputs and outputs) involved in making the transitions.

PR:6.18		A Federal CKMS **shall** support at least the following key lifecycle states and protect transitions among them: active, deactivated, and compromised.

PA:6.6		A Federal CKMS **should** support the destroyed state.

PF:6.1		A Federal CKMS **could** support the following key lifecycle states and verify the integrity and acceptability of transitions among them: pre-activation and suspended.

6.4   Key and Metadata Management Functions

In an FCKMS, an entity can initiate key and metadata management functions. The functions themselves are performed entirely within an FCKMS module, which contains a cryptographic module to perform the cryptographic functions used by the FCKMS module. An Access Control System (ACS) (see Section 6.7.1) performs the authentication and authorization of an entity initiating a function.

An FCKMS should provide for the creation, modification, replacement, and destruction of keys and their metadata. Depending on the impact-level and key type, the input and/or output could have integrity authentication, source authentication, and/or confidentiality services applied to them.

A trusted channel is a protected communication link established between the cryptographic module and a sender or receiver to securely communicate unprotected plaintext CSPs, keys, and authentication data. A trusted channel protects its contents from unauthorized modification and disclosure along the communication link (see [ISO19790]).

A trusted channel exhibits a verification capability that permits the operator or the module to confirm that the trusted channel has been established. The trusted channel must use only NIST-approved security functions (see [FIPS 140]) to establish the channel and transfer data.

In the following subsections, the use of "key" applies to a symmetric key and an asymmetric key pair, as appropriate, unless otherwise indicated.

Parameters for a cryptographic function should be verified during input to an FCKMS and a cryptographic module by verifying the protections (e.g., integrity codes) that have been placed on the parameters.

FR:6.17 The CKMS design **shall** specify the key and metadata management functions to be implemented and supported.

FR:6.18 The CKMS design **shall** identify the integrity, confidentiality, and source authentication services that are applied to each key and metadata management function parameter implemented in the CKMS.

PR:6.19		A Federal CKMS **shall** support all key and metadata management functions that are required by the FCKMS Security Policy.
PR:6.20		For Moderate and High impact-level systems, all sensitive data **shall** be transferred by means of a trusted channel.

PA:6.7		A Federal CKMS **should** support the following key and metadata management functions: generate a key, deactivate a key, register an owner, revoke a key, associate a key with its metadata, list key metadata, destroy a key and its metadata, establish a key, validate a key, recover a key and its metadata, and perform cryptographic functions using a key and its metadata.
PA:6.8		A Federal CKMS **should** support the following for all user requests for key-management services: a) The authentication of the identity/role of the entity initiating the request, and b) A verification of the requestor's authorization for receiving the service.
PA:6.9		For Low impact-level systems, all sensitive data **should** be transferred by means of a trusted channel.

6.4.1 Generate a Key

When an entity requires a key, and it is not automatically provided by an FCKMS, the entity should request that a key be generated by the FCKMS. The entity may need to specify the type of key and other necessary information (e.g., the name of the key-generation technique), including some metadata that needs to be associated with the key when requesting this function. The function may not return the newly generated key, but could, for example, return a key identifier that points to the key and its associated metadata.

Key-generation techniques typically depend on the cryptographic algorithm that will be used with the key and the use of a random number generator. Different algorithms use keys that have differing specifications (e.g., lengths and formats). Key generation for an asymmetric algorithm results in the generation of a key pair, rather than a single key, which is the case for symmetric algorithms. NIST has approved several random number generators (see [SP 800-90A], [SP 800-90B], [SP 800-90C] and [SP 800-131A]) and specifications for key generation (see [SP 800-133]).

The key-generation function could provide, or require the input of, metadata that is to be associated with the generated key.

FR:6.19 The CKMS design **shall** specify the key generation methods to be used in the CKMS for each type of key.

FR:6.20 The CKMS design **shall** specify the underlying random number generators that are used to generate symmetric and private keys.

| PR:6.21 | | A Federal CKMS **shall** support and use NIST-approved methods for key generation. |

PR:6.22		A Federal CKMS **shall** generate keys using a NIST-approved random number generator that provides a security strength that meets or exceeds the security strength required for the key.

6.4.2 Register an Owner

The initial registration of a security entity (i.e., an individual (person), organization, device or process) and a cryptographic key with metadata is a fundamental requirement of every FCKMS. This requirement is difficult to fully automate while preserving security (i.e., protecting from an impersonation threat), and thus, it usually requires verified and authorized human interactions. There typically exists a registration process in an FCKMS that associates each entity's initial set of long-term (i.e., static) secret, public, and/or private keys with the entity's identifier and perhaps other metadata. The process of associating a key-owner's identifier, key, and metadata involves either an initial identity-based authentication by a human relying on specific identification information, or relying on the pre-existing identity of the owner in some FCKMS.

FR:6.21 The CKMS design **shall** specify all the processes involved in owner registration, including the process for binding keys with the owner's identifier.

PR:6.23	IA-4	A Federal CKMS **shall**: a) Support the initial registration and periodic verification of each security entity that is to be managed, b) Manage the association of each security entity with its key and its associated metadata, and c) Provide owner registration and key association processes that can be implemented and evaluated for all FCKMS entities.
PR:6.24	IA-4	During a registration process, a Federal CKMS **shall** register a security entity, as well as the entity's initial cryptographic keys and metadata.

6.4.3 Activate a Key

The activation function provides for the transition of a cryptographic key from the pre-activation state to the active state (see [SP 800-57 Part 1] for further information). A key could be automatically activated immediately after generation, upon request, or in accordance with a date-time metadata value (e.g., set at the time of key generation) that indicates when the key needs to become active and can be used.

FR:6.22 The CKMS design **shall** specify how each key type is activated and the circumstances for activating the key.

FR:6.23 For each key type, the CKMS design **shall** specify requirements for the notification of key activation, including which parties are notified, how they are notified, what security services are applied to the notification, and the time-frames for notification(s).

6.4.4 Deactivate a Key

This function transitions a key from an active state to a deactive state (see [SP 800-57 Part 1] for further information). A cryptographic key is generally given a deactivation date and time when it is created and distributed. Deactivation may also be based on the number of times a key has been used to apply cryptographic protection or the amount of data that it has been used to protect. This period usually has a maximum value, based in part on the impact-levels of the data that the key is protecting and the threats that could be brought against that key or the entire FCKMS.

FR:6.24 The CKMS design **shall** specify, for each key type, how deactivation of the key is determined (e.g., by crypto period, by number of uses, or by the amount of data).

FR:6.25 The CKMS design **shall** specify how each key type is deactivated (e.g., manually or automatically, based on the deactivation date-time, the number of usages, or the amount of protected data).

FR:6.26 The CKMS design **shall** specify how the deactivation date-time for each key type can be changed.

FR:6.27 For each key type, the CKMS design **shall** specify requirements for advance notification of the deactivation of the key type, including which CKMS supported roles are notified, how they are notified, what security services are applied to the notification, and the time-frames for notification(s).

PR:6.25		A Federal CKMS **shall** support deactivating an active symmetric or private key and notifying relying parties that the key has been deactivated.

6.4.5 Revoke a Key

When a key is to be removed from service, it may be revoked. Key revocation should be used when the authorized use of a key must be terminated prior to the end of its cryptoperiod. A cryptographic key should be revoked as soon as feasible after its use is no longer authorized (e.g., the key has been compromised). Entities that have been, are, or will be using the key (i.e., relying parties) need to be notified that the key has been revoked. Such notification is accomplished by sending the notification to all relying parties and/or providing a notification that can be accessed by the relying parties, when needed. In this publication, revocation applies to both symmetric and asymmetric keys.

FR:6.28 The CKMS design **shall** specify when, how, and under what circumstances revocation is performed and revocation information is made available to the relying parties.

PR:6.26		A Federal CKMS **shall** support the revocation of a key and maintaining the reason for revocation.
PR:6.27		A Federal CKMS **shall** provide a notification when a key is revoked, including the reason for the revocation.

6.4.6 Suspend and Re-Activate a Key

A key may be temporarily suspended and later re-activated, i.e., suspension is a temporary revocation of the key. While revocation is generally irreversible, suspension can be reversed. Entities that may be using or relying on a key must be notified of both the suspension and the re-activation of the key.

Situations that may warrant suspension of a key, rather than irreversible revocation, include: the unavailability of the owner for an extended period of time, a misuse of the key, a possible compromise that is under investigation, and the misplacement of a token containing the key.

FR:6.29 The CKMS design **shall** specify how, and under what circumstances, a key can be suspended.

FR:6.30 The CKMS design **shall** specify how suspension information is made available to the relying or communicating parties.

FR:6.31 The CKMS design **shall** specify how, and under what circumstances, a suspended key is re-activated.

FR:6.32 The CKMS design **shall** specify how the suspended key is prevented from performing security services.

FR:6.33 The CKMS design **shall** specify how re-activation information is made available to the relying or communicating parties.

PR:6.28		When a key is suspended, a Federal CKMS **shall** provide a notification to all relying parties, including the reason for the suspension.
PR:6.29		When a key is re-activated after a suspension, a Federal CKMS **shall** provide a notification to all relying parties.

PF:6.2		A Federal CKMS **could** be capable of suspending and reactivating a key.

6.4.7 Renew a Public Key Certificate

Public key certificates contain the public key of an asymmetric key pair and a validity period for that certificate. Renewal establishes a new validity period by issuing a new certificate containing the same public key, but a new validity period.

The public key in a certificate corresponds to a private key (which is kept secret). One key of the key pair is used to apply cryptographic protection (e.g., to generate a digital signature), and the other key is used to process the protected information (e.g., to verify a digital signature). Each key of the key pair has its own cryptoperiod. The cryptoperiod of a key used to apply protection can be considered as being the "originator usage period," and the cryptoperiod of a key used to process the protected information can be considered to be the "recipient usage period." The validity period in a certificate applies to the key that is used to apply protection, and must not exceed the key's originator usage period.

Several algorithms have been approved that use key pairs, and the role of each key of the key pair is not necessarily the same. See [SP 800-57 Part 1] for more information.

- For digital signature key pairs, the private key is used to generate the signature (i.e., apply protection), so it would have an originator usage period; the public key is used to verify the signature (i.e., process the protected information), so it would have a recipient usage period. The validity period in a certificate pertains to the use of the private key.

- For key transport keys, the public key is used to apply protection (i.e., encrypt), so its cryptoperiod would be considered as an originator usage period, while the private key is used to decrypt, so it's cryptoperiod would be considered as the recipient usage period. In this case, the originator usage period pertains to the use of the public key.

- For key agreement algorithms, the cryptoperiods of the two keys of the key pair are usually the same.

The sum of the validity periods for the original certificate and all renewed certificates for the same key must not exceed the cryptoperiod of the key used to apply protection (i.e., the key with the originator usage period).

An FCKMS could notify the owner of a certificate when a certificate is about to expire so that the certificate could be renewed prior to the end validity date on the certificate.

FR:6.34 The CKMS design **shall** specify how and the conditions under which a public key can be renewed.

FR:6.35 For each key type, the CKMS design **shall** specify requirements for advance notification of the key type renewal, including which parties are notified, how they are notified, what security services are applied to the notification, and the time-frames for notification(s).

PR:6.30		A Federal CKMS **shall not** renew the validity period of a public key certificate beyond the cryptoperiod of the key of the key pair used to apply cryptographic protection (i.e., the originator usage period).

PF:6.3		A Federal CKMS **could** notify the owner of a public-key certificate that the certificate is about to expire.
PF:6.4		A Federal CKMS **could** provide notification to the relying parties of a public key certificate that the certificate has been renewed.

6.4.8   Key Derivation or Key Update

When a key is derived from other information (some of which is secret) in a non-reversible manner, the process is called key derivation. Key update is a special case of key derivation in which the secret information includes a symmetric key (K_1), and the derived symmetric key (K_2) replaces K_1 for the next key-update process. Key updating could result in a security exposure if an adversary obtains a key and knows the update process used. Key update is not supported in this Profile.

FR:6.36 The CKMS design **shall** specify all processes used to derive or update keys and the circumstances under which the keys are derived or updated.

FR:6.37 For each key type, the CKMS design **shall** specify requirements for advance notification for deriving or updating the keys, including which parties are notified, how they are notified, what security services are applied to the notification, and the time-frames for notification(s).

PR:6.31		A Federal CKMS **shall not** support key update.
PR:6.32		A Federal CKMS **shall** use only NIST-approved or allowed key derivation methods.

6.4.9   Destroy a Key and Metadata

When a key and its sensitive metadata are no longer to be used for normal operations, then all copies residing in operational storage (including within a cryptographic module) and in backup storage should be destroyed as soon as possible. Keys and sensitive metadata in an archive should be destroyed when no longer needed. Non-sensitive metadata may be retained for administrative purposes.

This Profile considers this function to be a local function, destroying only locally stored keys upon request. Destroying keys in remote locations may require special messages that request a key's destruction.

FR:6.38 The CKMS design **shall** specify how and the circumstances under which keys are intentionally destroyed and whether the destruction is local or universal throughout the CKMS.

FR:6.39 For each key type, the CKMS design **shall** specify requirements for an advance notification of key destruction, including which parties are notified, how they are notified, what security services are applied to the notification, and the time-frames for notification(s).

PR:6.33		When a key and/or its sensitive metadata are no longer to be used, a Federal CKMS **shall** destroy all local copies of the key and/or its sensitive metadata.

PR:6.34		When keys and sensitive metadata reside in remote locations, a means for requesting their destruction **shall** be available that provides integrity protection and source authentication.
PR:6.35	SC-12	When keys are destroyed, the Federal CKMS **shall** employ an approved key destruction method.
PR:6.36		When sensitive metadata is destroyed, the Federal CKMS **shall** employ an approved metadata destruction method.

6.4.10 Associate a Key with its Metadata

A cryptographic key could have several metadata elements associated with it. The CKMS designer determines which metadata are to be associated with a key and selects the protection mechanism(s) that provide(s) the association. Depending on the sensitivity of a metadata element, the metadata element could require confidentiality protection, integrity protection, and source authentication. The association function uses cryptography or a trusted process to provide these protections.

FR:6.40 For each key type used, the CKMS design **shall** specify what metadata is associated with the key, how the metadata is associated with the key, and the circumstances under which metadata is associated with the key.

FR:6.41 For each key type used, the CKMS design **shall** describe how the following security services (protections) are applied to the associated metadata: source authentication, integrity, and confidentiality.

PR:6.37		A Federal CKMS **shall**: a) Create a trusted association between a key and its metadata upon their entry into the FCKMS, b) Maintain the trusted association throughout the key's lifetime, and c) Establish a new trusted association following modification or replacement of any metadata.
PR:6.38		A Federal CKMS that protects Moderate or High impact-level information **shall** cryptographically bind a key and its metadata elements.

PA:6.10		A Federal CKMS that protects Low impact-level information **should** cryptographically bind a key and its metadata elements.

6.4.11 Modify Metadata

The modify metadata function can be used to modify existing metadata that is associated with a key. Some metadata elements for a key type may be fixed after creation and not modifiable; other metadata elements may by modified by some entities, but not by others. Attempted unauthorized modification of metadata that are associated with a key must be detected, prevented, and should be reported.

FR:6.42 The CKMS design **shall** specify the circumstances under which associated metadata is modified.

PR:6.39		A Federal CKMS **shall** designate which metadata elements are modifiable by authorized entities and which metadata elements cannot be modified after initial creation.
PR:6.40	AC-3	A Federal CKMS **shall** prevent the modification of metadata except by authorized entities.

PA:6.11		A Federal CKMS **should** report the attempted modification of metadata by unauthorized entities to the system administrator.

6.4.12 Delete Metadata

This function deletes metadata associated with a key. A deletion of the metadata requires the authentication of the requestor and verification of his/her authorization. Metadata elements may be deleted as an entire group, as an individual element, or as a specific subset of the elements.

FR:6.43 The CKMS design **shall** specify the circumstances under which the metadata associated with a key is deleted.

FR:6.44 The CKMS design **shall** specify the technique used to delete associated metadata.

PR:6.41	AC-3	A Federal CKMS **shall** allow metadata destruction only by authenticated and authorized entities.
PR:6.42		A Federal CKMS **shall** support the selection of metadata elements to be destroyed and the designation of who is authorized to perform the destruction.

6.4.13 List Key Metadata

This function allows an authorized entity to list one or more metadata elements of a key. The authorization of an entity to use a key does not automatically authorize that entity to list the key's metadata elements. Each metadata element could be assigned with a different set of permissions (e.g., some metadata elements could be prohibited from being listed at all), others could be listed by any user, while still others could be listed by only persons assuming a particular role (e.g., an administrator or auditor).

FR:6.45 For each key type, the CKMS design **shall** specify which metadata can be listed by authorized entities.

PR:6.43		A Federal CKMS **shall** provide metadata elements only to those entities authenticated and authorized for access to them.

6.4.14 Store Operational Key and Metadata Outside a Cryptographic Module

This function involves placing a key and/or metadata in storage outside of a cryptographic module for use during the key's cryptoperiod without retaining the original copy in the cryptographic module (as opposed to a copy function, where the key resides in two locations). Keys and metadata must be physically or cryptographically protected when stored outside a cryptographic module (see the requirements specified in Section 6.1.2, Section 6.2.1, and [SP 800-57 Part 1]).

FR:6.46 For each key type, the CKMS design **shall** specify: the circumstances under which keys of each type and their metadata are stored, where the keys and metadata are stored, and how the keys and metadata are protected.

6.4.15 Backup of a Key and its Metadata

The backup of keys and metadata involves copying the keys and/or metadata to a separate medium than is used for the operational storage of keys and from which the keys can be recovered if the original (operational) copy is lost, modified, or otherwise becomes unavailable. The FCKMS, the owner, or a trusted entity could back up keys and metadata.

FR:6.47 The CKMS design **shall** specify how, where, and the circumstances under which keys and their metadata are backed up.

FR:6.48 The CKMS design **shall** specify the security policy for the protection of backed-up keys/metadata.

FR:6.49 The CKMS design **shall** specify how the security policy is implemented during the key and metadata back up, e.g., how the confidentiality and multiparty control requirements are implemented during transport and storage of the backed-up keys and metadata.

PR:6.44	CP-6 CP-9	When keys and metadata are backed up, a medium that is separate from that used for the operational storage of the keys and metadata **shall** be used.
PR:6.45	SC-28	A Federal CKMS **shall** provide backed up keys and metadata with the same integrity and confidentiality protections as the operational copies of the keys and metadata and at the same or higher security strength.

6.4.16 Archive Key and/or Metadata

Key and/or metadata archiving involves placing a copy of a key and/or metadata in a safe storage facility so that they can be recovered if and when needed. Key and/or metadata archiving includes provisions for moving the key and/or metadata to a new storage medium before the old medium is replaced or becomes unreadable.

An archive should support the FCKMS Security Policy (see Section 4.3) in archive facilities and when moving keys and metadata to and from an archive. Archived keys and/or metadata must be physically or cryptographically protected. Keys used to protect archived keys and/or metadata will have cryptoperiods, and must be replaced when their cryptoperiods expire. Changing an archive key may involve changing to a stronger cryptographic algorithm and archive key, and re-encryption of the archived keys and/or metadata under the new archive key and algorithm.

Maintaining a key and metadata archive could require moving archived keys and/or metadata to new storage media when the old media are no longer readable because of the aging of, or technical changes to, the media and media readers. When the archived keys and/or metadata have been transferred to a new storage medium, the copies on the old storage medium must be destroyed (see [SP 800-88]).

FR:6.50 The CKMS design **shall** specify how, where, and the circumstances under which keys and/or their metadata are archived.

FR:6.51 The CKMS design **shall** specify the technique for the secure destruction of the key and/or metadata or the secure destruction of the old storage medium after being written onto a new storage medium.

FR:6.52 The CKMS design **shall** specify how keys and/or their metadata are protected after the cryptoperiod of an archive key expires.

PR:6.46	SC-28	When keys and metadata are archived, a Federal CKMS **shall** provide them with the same integrity and confidentiality protections as the operational copies of the keys and metadata and at the same, or a higher, security strength.
PR:6.47	SI-12	When keys and metadata are archived, a Federal CKMS **shall** archive keys and metadata in accordance with applicable laws, regulations, and policies.
PR:6.48		When archived keys and metadata are moved to a new medium, a Federal CKMS **shall** destroy the copies of keys and metadata on the old storage medium using approved methods.

PA:6.12		A Federal CKMS **should** archive long-term keys and metadata in accordance with [SP 800-57 Part 1].
PA:6.13		A Federal CKMS **should** move archived keys and metadata to an alternate readable storage medium before the old medium is replaced or becomes unreadable.

6.4.17 Recover a Key and/or Metadata

Key and/or metadata recovery involves obtaining a copy of a key and/or its metadata that has been previously backed up or archived. The key and/or metadata must be recovered by an authorized entity (e.g., its owner or a key-recovery agent) following the rules for recovery stated in the FCKMS Security Policy and in accordance with Section 6.1.2 and Section 6.2.1.

FR:6.53 The CKMS design **shall** specify the CKMS recovery policy for keys and/or metadata.

FR:6.54 The CKMS design **shall** specify the mechanisms used to implement and enforce the recovery policy for keys and/or metadata.

FR:6.55 The CKMS design **shall** specify how, and the circumstances under which, keys and/or metadata are recovered from each key database or metadata storage facility.

FR:6.56 The CKMS design **shall** specify how keys and/or metadata are protected during recovery.

PR:6.49		A Federal CKMS **shall** support recovering keys and/or metadata that have been backed up or archived, following the FCKMS rules for recovery.

6.4.18 Establish a Key

Key establishment is the process by which a key is securely shared between two or more entities. The key may be transported from one entity to another (key transport), or the key may be derived from a shared secret generated by the entities (key agreement). The method of transporting or sharing keys may be either manual (e.g., sent by a courier) or automated (e.g., sent over the Internet).

FR:6.57 The CKMS design **shall** specify how, and the circumstances under which, keys and their metadata are established.

6.4.19 Enter a Key and Associated Metadata into a Cryptographic Module

The key-entry function of a cryptographic module is used to enter one or more keys and associated metadata into the module in preparation for use by the module. Section 2.10 above requires the use of FIPS-140-validated cryptographic modules and relates the impact-levels of data requiring protection to the [FIPS 140] security levels.

FR:6.58 The CKMS design **shall** specify how, and the circumstances under which, keys and metadata are entered into a cryptographic module, the form in which they are entered, and the method used for entry.

FR:6.59 The CKMS design **shall** specify how the integrity and confidentiality (if necessary) of the entered keys and metadata are protected and verified upon entry.

PR:6.50		A Federal CKMS **shall** enter keys into cryptographic modules in accordance with the requirements in [FIPS 140] and the impact-levels associated with the keys.

| PR:6.51 | | A Federal CKMS **shall** enter sensitive metadata into cryptographic modules in accordance with the [FIPS 140] requirements for the entry of sensitive security parameters. |
| PR:6.52 | | A Federal CKMS operating at the Moderate or High impact-levels **shall** enter keys and/or sensitive metadata into cryptographic modules by means of a trusted channel. |

| PA:6.14 | | A Federal CKMS operating at the Low impact-level **should** enter keys and/or sensitive metadata into cryptographic modules by means of a trusted channel that employs either identity-based authentication or role-based authentication of the sending and receiving entities. |

6.4.20 Output a Key and Associated Metadata from a Cryptographic Module

The key-output function of a cryptographic module outputs one or more keys and their associated metadata from the module. The output of keys and metadata could be needed in order to store (outside the cryptographic module), transfer, back up, or archive them. A cryptographic module that serves as a key-generation facility for other FCKMS modules would output keys prior to distribution.

As with key entry, a trusted channel is either required or recommended for key and sensitive data output, depending on the impact-level of the system.

FR:6.60 The CKMS design **shall** specify how, and the circumstances under which, keys and metadata can be output from a cryptographic module and the form in which they are output.

FR: 6.61 The CKMS design **shall** specify how the confidentiality and integrity of the output keys and metadata are protected while outside of a cryptographic module.

FR:6.62 If a private key, symmetric key, or confidential metadata is output from the cryptographic module in plaintext form, the CKMS design **shall** specify if and how the calling entity is authenticated before the key and metadata are provided.

PR:6.53		A Federal CKMS **shall** output keys from cryptographic modules in accordance with the requirements in [FIPS 140] and the impact-levels associated with the keys.
PR:6.54		A Federal CKMS **shall** output sensitive metadata from cryptographic modules in accordance with the [FIPS 140] requirements for the output of sensitive security parameters.
PR:6.55		A Federal CKMS operating at the Moderate or High impact-levels **shall** output keys and/or sensitive metadata from cryptographic modules by means of a trusted channel.

PA:6.15		A Federal CKMS operating at the Low impact-level **should** output keys and/or sensitive metadata from cryptographic modules by means of a trusted channel.

6.4.21 Validate Public-Key Domain Parameters

This function performs certain validity checks on the public domain parameters of some public-key algorithms (e.g., Diffie-Hellman key establishment and ECDSA).

FR:6.63 The CKMS design **shall** specify how, where, and the circumstances under which, public-key domain parameters are validated.

PR:6.56		For applicable public-key algorithms, a Federal CKMS **shall** validate a public key's domain parameters as specified in [SP 800-56A] or [SP 800-89] before using them.

6.4.22 Validate a Public Key

This function performs certain validity checks on a public key to provide some assurance that it is arithmetically correct.

FR:6.64 The CKMS design **shall** specify how, where, and the circumstances under which, public keys are validated.

PR:6.57		A Federal CKMS **shall** validate public keys as specified in [SP 800-56A], [SP 800-56B] or [SP 800-89] before using them.

6.4.23 Validate a Public Key Certification Path

This function validates the certification path (also known as a certificate chain) from the relying entity's trust anchor[5] to a public key in which the relying entity needs to establish trust (i.e., the public key of the other entity in a transaction). Validation of the certification path provides assurance that the identity of the originating entity, as specified in the certificate, is the owner of the public key in the certificate and is the holder of the corresponding private key. The latter assumes that a trusted certificate authority obtained proof of private-key possession.

FR:6.65 The CKMS design **shall** specify how, where, and the circumstances under which, a key certification path is validated.

PR:6.58	IA-5 (2)	A Federal CKMS **shall** validate the certification path of a public key certificate prior to using the public key in the certificate.

---

[5] Technically, a trust anchor is a CA with a trusted certificate containing the CA's public key. However, the term is also commonly used to refer to that certificate, which is usually cached locally in a trust-anchor store. In this document, the term refers to a certificate.

6.4.24 Validate a Symmetric Key

This function performs a validity check on a symmetric key, e.g., to verify that the length and format are correct. The function could also verify any error detection/correction codes or integrity checks placed upon the key and/or its metadata.

FR:6.66 The CKMS design **shall** specify how, where, and the circumstances under which symmetric keys and/or metadata are validated.

PR:6.59		A Federal CKMS **shall** validate a symmetric key before its initial use.

6.4.25 Validate Possession of a Symmetric Key

This function is used by an entity who receives an encrypted symmetric key and who needs assurance that the claimed sender of the key has possession of the plaintext key. This assurance may be obtained by encapsulating the plaintext key in a key package that has sufficient redundancy known by the receiver. The receiver verifies the redundancy after decryption. Alternatively, the sender and receiver may undergo a handshake that provides assurance that the sender possesses the correct key.

PR:6.60		A Federal CKMS **shall** obtain assurance of symmetric key possession by the sender of a symmetric key.

6.4.26 Validate a Private Key (or Key Pair)

This function performs tests on private keys or key pairs to verify that they meet their specifications. Only the private-key owner or a trusted third party acting on behalf of the private-key owner can perform this test.

FR:6.67 The CKMS design **shall** specify how, where and the circumstances under which, private keys or key pairs and/or metadata can be validated.

PR:6.61		A Federal CKMS **shall** validate private keys or key pairs as specified in [SP 800-56A] or [SP 800-56B] before their first use.

6.4.27 Validate the Possession of a Private Key

This function is used by an entity that receives a public key and needs assurance that the claimed owner of the public key has possession of the corresponding private key.

FR:6.68 The CKMS design **shall** specify how, where, and the circumstances under which, possession of private keys and their metadata are validated.

PR:6.62		Assurance of private-key possession by the key's owner **shall be** obtained before its first use as specified in [SP 800-56A], [SP 800-56B] or [SP 800-89].

6.4.28 Perform a Cryptographic Function using the Key

Cryptographic functions using keys are performed in a cryptographic module to cryptographically protect data, including metadata and other keys, and process already-protected information. These functions may include signature generation, signature verification, data encryption, ciphertext decryption, key wrapping, key unwrapping, MAC generation, and MAC verification.

FR:6.69 The CKMS design **shall** specify all cryptographic functions that are supported and where they are performed in the CKMS (e.g., CA, host, or end user system).

6.4.29 Manage the Trust Anchor Store

An FCKMS could require that some entities have one or more trusted public keys, called "trust anchors[6]." Trust anchors are cached in a trust anchor store. A trust anchor can be used to establish trust in other public keys that might not otherwise be trusted. Therefore, the integrity of trust anchors is critical to the security of the FCKMS. The FCKMS typically supports trust-anchor management functions, such as adding, deleting and storing trust anchors.

Many commonly used products, such as browsers, are delivered and initially installed with an assortment of trust anchors, not all of which merit trust.

FR:6.70 The CKMS design **shall** specify all trust anchor management functions that are supported (see RFC 6024).

FR:6.71 The CKMS design **shall** specify how the trust anchors are securely distributed so that the relying parties can perform source authentication and integrity verification on those trust anchors.

FR:6.72 The CKMS design **shall** specify how the trust anchors are managed in relying-entity systems to ensure that only authorized additions, modifications, and deletions are made to the relying-entity system's trust anchor store.

PR:6.63	SC-12	A Federal CKMS **shall** only use trust anchors that meet the following conditions: a) The organization associated with the trust anchor is trusted, b) The security policy associated with the trust anchor is acceptable, c) The actual source of the trust anchor has been authenticated, and d) The integrity of the trust anchor has been verified.
PR:6.64		Only authorized additions, modifications, and deletions **shall** be made to trust anchors within an FCKMS.

---

[6] As used here, "trust anchor" refers to the certificate of a trusted CA, rather than to the CA itself.

| PA:6.16 | | A Federal CKMS **should** use trust anchor formats as specified in [RFC 5914] or its revisions. |

6.5 Cryptographic Key and/or Metadata Security: In Storage

Cryptographic keys are typically stored with their metadata. An FCKMS should verify the authorization of the submitting entity and the integrity of the submitted key and metadata before they are stored. For Moderate and High impact-level systems, identity-based authentication is required, and for Low impact-level systems either identity-based or role based authentication is required. See Section 6.5 of the Framework for further discussion.

An FCKMS must only allow authorized users to have access to stored keys. Thus, an Access Control System (ACS) (see Section 6.7.1) should protect stored keys and metadata.

FR:6.73 The CKMS design **shall** specify the methods used to authenticate the identity and verify the authorization of the entity submitting keys and/or metadata for storage.

FR:6.74 The CKMS design **shall** specify the methods used to verify the integrity of keys and/or metadata submitted for storage.

FR:6.75 The CKMS design **shall** specify the methods used to protect the confidentiality of symmetric and private stored keys and metadata.

FR:6.76 If a key-wrapping key (or key pair) is used to protect stored keys, then the CKMS design **shall** specify the methods used to protect the key-wrapping key (or key pair) and control its use.

FR:6.77 The CKMS design **shall** specify the methods used to protect the integrity of stored keys and metadata.

FR:6.78 The CKMS design **shall** specify how access to stored keys is controlled.

FR:6.79 The CKMS design **shall** specify the techniques used for correcting or recovering all stored keys.

PR:6.65	AC-3	Before keys and metadata are stored or retrieved from storage, a Federal CKMS **shall** verify the authorization of the entity submitting or requesting keys and/or metadata.
PR:6.66		A Federal CKMS supporting Moderate or High impact-level systems **shall** support identity-based authentication in order to verify the identity and authorization of the entity making a key or metadata storage or retrieval request.
PR:6.67		A Federal CKMS supporting Low impact-level systems **shall** support either identity-based authentication or role-based authentication in order to verify the authorization of the entity

		making a key or metadata storage or retrieval request.
PR:6.68		A Federal CKMS **shall** verify the integrity of keys and metadata before they are stored or retrieved from storage.

6.6 Cryptographic Key and Metadata Security: During Key Establishment

Keys and metadata can be established between entities needing to communicate securely using key transport or key agreement methods. These methods are typically used to establish keys over electronic communications networks, but some of these could also be used to provide extra security (i.e., beyond physical protection) when keys are manually distributed. [SP 800-56A] and [SP 800-56B] specify cryptographic schemes for automated key establishment. PR:2.2 in Section 2.2 requires the use of NIST-approved key-establishment schemes for automated key establishment.

6.6.1 Key Transport

When symmetric or private cryptographic keys and sensitive metadata are transported (distributed) from one entity (the sender) to one or more other entities (the intended receiver(s)), they must be protected. Symmetric keys and private keys require confidentiality protection, and all keys require integrity protection. A trusted courier can physically protect a manually transported key, while automated electronic-based transport must be protected using cryptography. NIST-approved methods for automated key transport are provided in [SP 800-56A] and [SP 800-56B].

The receiver of a transported key typically needs assurance that the key came from the expected, authorized key sender. When transported using automated methods, this assurance may be provided by a cryptographic mechanism (which is part of the complete key-establishment protocol) that authenticates the identity of the sender to the receiver; the FCKMS should verify the sender's authority to perform the transport. When a key is transported manually, authenticating the identity of the courier, and verifying the courier's authorization to transport the key should be used to provide this assurance.

FR:6.80 The CKMS design **shall** specify the methods used to protect the confidentiality of symmetric and private keys during their transport.

FR:6.81 The CKMS design **shall** specify the methods used to protect the integrity of transported keys and how the keys can be reconstructed or replaced after detecting errors.

FR:6.82 The CKMS design **shall** specify how the identity of the key sender is authenticated to the receiver of transported keying material.

PR:6.69		When keys and metadata are received using a key-transport scheme, a Federal CKMS **shall** support mechanisms to verify: a) The authorization of the source, b) The integrity of the received data, and

		c) That confidentiality has been provided to secret and private keys and sensitive metadata.

6.6.2 Key Agreement

Two entities working together can create and agree on a cryptographic key without the key being transported from one entity to the other during an automated key-agreement process. Cryptographic algorithms employing key-agreement keys are used by each entity. NIST-approved methods for key agreement using public-key algorithms are provided in [SP 800-56A] and [SP 800-56B].

Each entity participating in a key-agreement process must obtain assurance of the identity of the other entity during the execution of that process.

FR:6.83 The CKMS design **shall** specify each key agreement scheme supported by the CKMS.

FR:6.84 The CKMS design **shall** specify how each entity participating in a key agreement is authenticated.

PR:6.70		When keys and metadata are agreed-upon during an automated key-agreement process in a Federal CKMS, each entity involved in the transaction **shall** obtain assurance of the identity or role of the other party.

6.6.3 Key Confirmation

When keys are established between two entities, each entity should confirm that the other entity did, in fact, have the correct key. [SP 800-56A] and [SP 800-56B] specify key confirmation schemes for use in some automated key-establishment schemes. Other methods may also be appropriate, such as decrypting ciphertext and comparing with the expected plaintext value.

FR:6.85 The CKMS design **shall** specify each key confirmation method used to confirm that the correct key was established with the other entity.

FR:6.86 The CKMS design **shall** specify the circumstances under which each key confirmation is performed.

PR:6.71		For Moderate and High impact-level systems, a Federal CKMS **shall** support key confirmation for all key-establishment transactions.

PA:6.17		For Low impact-level systems, a Federal CKMS **should** support key confirmation for all key-establishment transactions.

6.6.4   Key-Establishment Protocols

Several protocols have been developed for the establishment of cryptographic keys. Often, these protocols are designed for a particular application or set of applications (e.g., secure email or secure data file transfer).

A high-level overview of several key-establishment protocols can be found in [SP 800-57 Part 3], along with guidance as to which cryptographic options are recommended for U.S. Government use. In this document (i.e., SP 800-152), these protocols are referred to as NIST-allowed key-establishment protocols.

FR:6.87 The CKMS design **shall** specify all the protocols that are employed by the CKMS for key establishment and storage purposes.

PR:6.72		When key establishment is required, a Federal CKMS **shall** use a NIST-allowed key-establishment protocol.

6.7   Restricting Access to Key and Metadata Management Functions

Access to an FCKMS's key and metadata management functions should be supported for authorized entities and controlled to prevent unauthorized access to keys and metadata. An entity requesting an FCKMS service or initiating a cryptographic function should be authenticated, and that entity's authorization should be verified (see the Section 5 requirements).

6.7.1   The Access Control System (ACS)

An access control system is needed by an FCKMS to assure that every key and metadata management function can only be initiated by the FCKMS itself or in response to a request by an authorized entity. When key-management functions are initiated by an entity, an access control system must assure that the initiator is authenticated (i.e., by means of identity-based authentication or role-based authentication), performing only the requested functions that are authorized, and that all applicable constraints are satisfied. See Section 6.7.1 of the Framework for additional discussion.

FR:6.88 The CKMS design **shall** specify the topology of the CKMS by indicating the locations of the entities, the ACS, the function logic, and the connections between them.

FR:6.89 The CKMS design **shall** specify the constraints on the key management functions that are implemented to assure proper operation.

FR:6.90 The CKMS design **shall** specify how access to the key management functions is restricted to authorized entities.

FR:6.91 The CKMS design **shall** specify the ACS and its policy for controlling access to key management functions.

FR:6.92 The CKMS design **shall** specify at a minimum:

  a) The granularity of the entities (e.g., person, device, organization),

b) If and how entities are identified,

c) If and how entities are authenticated,

d) If and how the entity authorizations are verified, and

e) The access control on each key management function.

FR:6.93 The CKMS design **shall** specify the capabilities of its ACS to accommodate, implement, and enforce the CKMS Security Policy.

PR:6.73	AC-3 AC-24	A Federal CKMS **shall** control access to, and the initiation of, all its key and metadata management services and functions, granting access to and permission to initiate a requested service or function only after verifying the authorization of the requesting entity to perform the requested service or function.

6.7.2 Restricting Cryptographic Module Entry and Output of Plaintext Keys

An FCKMS should minimize human access to plaintext keys. The primary need for keys to be in plaintext is when they are performing cryptographic functions within a cryptographic module. A major concern is the entry and output of plaintext secret and private keys into/from the cryptographic module.

Note that Section 6.4.19 addresses the entry of keys and metadata into a cryptographic module, and Section 6.4.20 addresses the output from the module.

Also, note that Section 6.1.2 requires that keys for Moderate and High impact-level systems be cryptographically protected from unauthorized disclosure when outside a cryptographic module, i.e., when outside the module, secret and private keys need to be encrypted, rather than in plaintext form. Therefore, the entry and output of plaintext secret and private keys is only allowed for Low impact-level systems. However, Section 6.1.2 also recommends that these keys be encrypted.

FR:6.94 The CKMS design **shall** specify the circumstances under which plaintext secret or plaintext private keys are entered into or output from a cryptographic module.

FR:6.95 If plaintext secret or plaintext private keys are entered into or output from any cryptographic module, then the CKMS design **shall** specify how the plaintext keys are protected and controlled outside of the cryptographic module.

FR:6.96 If plaintext secret or plaintext private keys are entered into or output from any cryptographic module, then the CKMS design **shall** specify how such actions are audited.

6.7.3 Controlling Human Input

If a key-management function requires that a human input a key or sensitive metadata, the human must accept responsibility for the accuracy and security of the input, as well as entering the input at the proper time or when the proper event occurs. Minimizing human

SP 800-152   A Profile for U.S. Federal CKMS

involvement during operations, resulting in a more transparent system, is usually more desirable and may be more secure.

FR:6.97 For each key and metadata management function, the CKMS design **shall** specify all human input parameters, their formats, and the actions to be taken by the CKMS if they are not provided.

PA:6.18		A Federal CKMS **should** minimize human involvement in entering and outputting keys and sensitive metadata to/from the FCKMS.

6.7.4   Multiparty Control

Certain FCKMS key-management functions could require multiparty control. Requiring k of n entities to be authorized by the FCKMS access-control system before the function is performed could provide multiparty control. Multiparty controls should be used when performing key-management functions for highly sensitive applications.

Of particular concern are the keys used by a Certificate Authority to sign certificates and any keys used by the FCKMS for self-protection (e.g., the keys used to access other keys within the FCKMS, such as the keys used to protect a database of keys).

FR:6.98 The CKMS design **shall** specify all functions that require multiparty control, specifying k and n for each function.

FR: 6.99 For each multiparty function, the CKMS design **shall** cite or specify any known rationale (logic, mathematics) as to why any k of the n entities can enable the desired function, but k-1 of the entities cannot.

PR:6.74	AC-3 (2)	A Federal CKMS **shall** support multiparty control for managing and using Certificate Authority keys in High impact-level systems.

PA:6.19	AC-3 (2)	A Federal CKMS **should** use multiparty control for managing and using Certificate Authority keys in Low and Moderate impact-level systems.
PA:6.20	AC-3	A Federal CKMS **should** use multiparty control for Security Domain Authority functions.

6.7.5   Key Splitting

Key splitting is a technique for establishing multiparty control of keys. When a highly sensitive key is required, the key is split into n key splits so that for some k ($k \leq n$), any k key splits of the key can be used to form the key, but having any $k-1$ key splits provides no knowledge of the key value. Each of the n key splits is then provided to one of n trusted entities so that the key cannot be formed unless k of the entities agree to take part. But if any

k-1 of the key splits are compromised, the key still could not be reconstructed by an attacker having the k-1 key splits.

FR: 6.100 The CKMS design **shall** specify all keys that are managed using key splitting techniques and **shall** specify n and k for each technique.

FR: 6.101 For each (n, k) key splitting technique used, the CKMS design **shall** specify how key splitting is done, and any known rationale (logic, mathematics) as to why any k of the n key splits can form the key, but k-1 of the key splits provide no information about the key.

PF:6.5		A Federal CKMS **could** use key splitting in order to implement multiparty control of keys.

6.8   Compromise Recovery

A compromise is the unauthorized disclosure, modification, substitution, or use of sensitive data (e.g., keys, metadata, or other security-related information) or the unauthorized modification of a security-related system, device or process in order to gain unauthorized access. An FCKMS should protect all keys and sensitive metadata so that they are not disclosed, modified, substituted or used by unauthorized parties. This requires that all components in the FCKMS remain secure.

However, since it is difficult to prevent all potential security problems that could arise from all possible threats, an FCKMS should be designed to detect potential compromises and unauthorized modifications, to mitigate their undesirable effects, to alert the appropriate parties of compromises, and to recover (or help recover) to a secure state if a compromise or unauthorized modification is discovered.

PR:6.75	CP-2 PL-1 PS-1	A Federal CKMS **shall** create and maintain a Compromise Recovery Plan for recovering from actual and suspected compromises of its security.
PR:6.76	CP-2	A Federal CKMS **shall** perform the following when a compromise is detected or suspected: a) Report the compromise to FCKMS management, b) Evaluate the compromise to determine its cause and scope, c) Institute compromise-mitigation measures to minimize key and/or metadata exposure, d) Institute corrective measures to prevent the recurrence of the compromise, and, e) Return the FCKMS to a secure operating state.

6.8.1   Key Compromise

Key compromise is the disclosure of a key or its sensitive metadata to one or more unauthorized entities, or the modification, substitution, or use of a cryptographic key or its sensitive metadata by one or more unauthorized entities. Depending on the key type and key usage, the compromise of a key could result in:

a) Loss of confidentiality,

b) Loss of integrity,

c) Loss of authentication,

d) Loss of non-repudiation, or

e) Some combination of these losses.

Note that a compromise of a secret or private key could result in a compromise of all the information protected by the key and access to all security services supported by the key. Also, note that the compromise of the sensitive metadata of a key may result in the compromise of the key (see Section 6.8.2).

A key compromise could be prevented, undetected, detected, or suspected. An FCKMS should be designed and operated to 1) prevent key compromises, 2) detect actual compromises, 3) support the analysis of suspected compromises, and 4) minimize the risks of undetected compromises. Establishing a cryptoperiod or usage limit for each key can reduce the exposure caused by an undetected compromise[7]. See Section 6.8.1 of the Framework for additional discussion.

A cryptographic key may be used for applying cryptographic protection (e.g., encryption or generating a digital signature) or processing cryptographically protected information (e.g., decryption or verifying a digital signature). For symmetric algorithms, the same key is used both to apply the protection and process the protected information. For public-key algorithms, one key of a key pair is often used to apply the protection, and the other is used to process the protected information; for public-key algorithms, key compromise is concerned with the disclosure or modification of the private key of the key pair. Keys or key pairs known or suspected of being compromised must not be used to apply cryptographic protection, but they may be used to process cryptographically protected information, if required and unmodified (e.g., for continuity of operations), and the risk of doing so is acceptable.

An FCKMS should have the ability to rapidly revoke a key (see Section 6.8.3), replace keys (both asymmetric and symmetric) and the ability to notify the relying parties (those who make use of the key) of a compromise. A mobile FCKMS device should have the capability of being deactivated remotely by the FCKMS management, and the sensitive keys and metadata within the device should be destroyed if possible.

FR:6.102 The CKMS design **shall** specify the range of acceptable cryptoperiods or usage limits of each type of key used by the system.

FR:6.103 For each key, a CKMS design **shall** specify the other key types that depend on the key for their security and how those dependent keys are to be replaced in the event of a compromise of the initial key.

---

[7] The usage of keys may be limited based on a criterion, such as the amount of data processed using the key.

FR:6.104 The CKMS design **shall** specify the means by which other compromised keys can be identified when a key is compromised. For example, when a key derivation key is compromised, how are the derived keys determined?

PR:6.77		A Federal CKMS **shall** revoke compromised keys.
PR:6.78		A Federal CKMS **shall not** use a key whose compromise is known or suspected to apply cryptographic protection.
PR:6.79		A Federal CKMS **shall** support reporting and investigating a key compromise.

PA:6.21		A Federal CKMS **should** destroy compromised keys.
PA:6.22	AC-17 (9) SC-7	A Federal CKMS **should** have the capability of remotely deactivating mobile FCKMS devices and destroying sensitive keys and metadata within those devices.
PA:6.23		A Federal CKMS **should** replace compromised/revoked keys with new keys and metadata when continuity of operations is required.
PA:6.24		A Federal CKMS **should not** use a key whose compromise is known or suspected to process cryptographically protected information.

6.8.2 Metadata Compromise

Some metadata may be considered sensitive, while other metadata is not. Metadata compromise refers only to the compromise of the sensitive metadata. Depending on the metadata element and how it is used, its compromise could result in the compromise of one or more keys and the data protected by those keys. If different keys have common sensitive metadata elements, then the compromise of one sensitive metadata element may compromise the data protected by each of the keys. Metadata elements that are sensitive to unauthorized modification should be cryptographically bound to their associated keys so that the integrity of the metadata can be easily verified. Metadata elements that are sensitive to disclosure should be physically or cryptographically protected.

FR:6.105 For each key type employed, the CKMS design **shall** specify which metadata elements are sensitive to compromise (confidentiality, integrity, or source).

FR:6.106 The CKMS design **shall** specify the potential security consequences, given the compromise (confidentiality, integrity or source) of each sensitive metadata element of a key.

FR:6.107 The CKMS design **shall** specify how each sensitive metadata element compromise can be remedied.

PR:6.80		A Federal CKMS **shall** revoke the key associated with compromised sensitive metadata.
PR:6.81		A Federal CKMS **shall** support reporting and investigating a compromise of sensitive metadata.

PA:6.25		A Federal CKMS **should** destroy the keys whose sensitive metadata has been compromised, and also destroy all the sensitive metadata associated with that key.

6.8.3　Key and Metadata Revocation

Keys could be revoked for a number of reasons, including key compromise, metadata compromise, and the termination of an employee or the employee's role within an organization. Additional information is provided in Section 6.8.3 of the Framework.

FR:6.108 A CKMS design **shall** specify the key revocation mechanism(s) and associated relying-entity notification mechanism(s) used or available for use.

6.8.4　Cryptographic Module Compromise

Since a cryptographic module contains plaintext keys at some point during its operation, physical access to, and compromise of, a cryptographic module could compromise the symmetric and private keys contained within the module, as well as any sensitive metadata contained in the module. This could lead to the loss of confidentiality and/or integrity of the keys and metadata.

Cryptographic modules could be compromised either physically (i.e., obtaining the keys by physical penetration of the cryptographic module enclosure) or by non-invasive methods (i.e., obtaining keys, or knowledge about the keys via some external action). Physical protection could be provided to the modules by enclosing them in a facility or a protected space where unauthorized access is prevented or where unauthorized access could be quickly detected. Some modules provide this protection at their cryptographic boundary (see [FIPS 140]). If any access to the contents of a cryptographic module is possible, then an access control system should restrict access to only authorized parties.

Following an actual or suspected cryptographic module compromise, a secure state of the module must be re-established before the module is returned to normal operation, or the module must be replaced. Following repair or replacement, the security and correct operation of a module should be tested and approved before it becomes operational.

FR:6.109 The CKMS design **shall** specify how physical and logical access to the cryptographic module contents is restricted to authorized entities.

FR:6.110 The CKMS design **shall** specify the approach to be used to recover from a cryptographic module compromise.

FR:6.111 The CKMS design **shall** describe what non-invasive attacks are mitigated by the cryptographic modules used by the system and provide a description of how the mitigation is performed.

FR:6.112 The CKMS design **shall** identify any cryptographic modules that are vulnerable to non-invasive attacks.

FR:6.113 The CKMS design **shall** provide the rationale for accepting the vulnerabilities caused by possible non-invasive attacks.

An FCKMS must use cryptographic modules that protect against unauthorized access to their contents (see Section 2.10 for requirements).

PR:6.82		A Federal CKMS **shall** repair or replace a compromised cryptographic module and then verify its correct operation and security before being used operationally.

6.8.5 Computer System Compromise Recovery

The security of an FCKMS often depends on the security and integrity of its own computer systems, including its hardware, software, and data. Unauthorized access to, or modifications of, any of these could corrupt secure computer operation. Unauthorized modification of FCKMS software or of a computer's operating system could be detected using tools that run on a separate secure platform and by monitoring any unauthorized modification to a file, changes to the hash value of a file's contents, or changes to a file's attributes. Alternatively, a layered system of protections could be built into the system; in this case, the mechanisms would need to be protected from the same threats as the system itself. When critical files undergo unauthorized modifications that are detected by the monitor or are indicated in the event log, then these files should be replaced with known valid and secure copies of those files obtained from secure backup storage.

An FCKMS could incorporate automated monitoring devices and software that detect certain threats or compromises. For example, some communication networks monitor for and detect errors that accidentally occur or have been induced in the network. If a network uses error-detection codes for communications, the monitor could detect error propagation characteristics that are outside the norm and initiate some compensating action to minimize the result of this type of compromise. If cryptographic-based Message Authentication Codes (MACs) are used in communications, certain deliberate and accidental modifications to the data (e.g., keys and metadata) can be detected. Non-cryptographic error-detection codes are not intended to detect deliberate modifications.

FR:6.114 The CKMS design **shall** specify the mechanisms used to detect unauthorized modifications to the CKMS system hardware, software and data.

FR:6.115 The CKMS design **shall** specify how the CKMS recovers from unauthorized modifications to the CKMS system hardware, software and data.

PR:6.83	CP-10	A Federal CKMS **shall** support the recovery of a system from backups after the detection of an unauthorized system modification.
PR:6.84		A Federal CKMS **shall** respond to a computer operating-system compromise as specified in the Compromise Recovery Plan.

PF:6.6		A Federal CKMS **could** automatically detect and report some compromise types, obtain upgrades that will deter or prevent similar future compromises, and then return the system to a known secure state.

6.8.6 Network Security Controls and Compromise Recovery

A compromise of any network security control that provides protection to the communications within an FCKMS could result in the compromise of the FCKMS itself, including its keys. See Section 6.8.6 of the Framework for additional information.

Whenever network security has been compromised, the incident should be fully investigated to determine what other systems and which keys may have been compromised due to the compromise of the network.

FR:6.116 The CKMS design **shall** specify how to recover from the compromise of the network security controls used by the system. Specifically,

a) The CKMS design **shall** specify the compromise scenarios considered for each network security control device,

b) The CKMS design **shall** specify which of the mitigation techniques specified in this section[8] are to be employed for each envisioned compromise scenario, and

c) The CKMS design **shall** specify any additional or alternative mitigation techniques that are to be employed.

PR:6.85		If network passwords are compromised, a Federal CKMS **shall**:
		a) Replace any passwords that are compromised or suspected of being compromised,
		b) Notify entities that may be affected by the compromise,
		c) Perform an assessment of any damage that could have resulted to the FCKMS, and
		d) Take corrective actions that would reduce the likelihood of similar failures.

---

[8] The mitigation techniques are provided in Section 6.8.6 of [SP 800-130], and also in **PR:6.84**, **PR:6.85** and **PA:6.26**.

PR:6.86		If the network security is compromised, a Federal CKMS **shall**: a) Investigate the cause of the compromise, b) Report the compromise to the system administrator, the CKMS designer, and/or the vendor of the compromised product, c) Determine the extent to which keys and metadata have been compromised (if possible), d) Install appropriate fixes so that the compromise will not reoccur, and e) Replace all compromised keys and sensitive metadata.

PA:6.26		A Federal CKMS **should** take corrective measures for network security compromises, including: a) Installing the latest network security patches, b) Changing network security devices if improved ones are available, c) Upgrading network security configurations, and d) Disabling obsolete or unused protocols.

6.8.7 Personnel Security Compromise Recovery

Anyone that is responsible for the secure operation of an FCKMS might have the capability to compromise its security. An FCKMS should be designed and operated with capabilities that minimize the likelihood of any successful human-initiated compromises, detect and minimize the negative consequences of the compromises, and efficiently recover from such compromises.

Any detected security failure should result in the initiation of recovery procedures, based upon the Information Security Policy and the FCKMS capabilities.

FR:6.117 The CKMS design **shall** specify any personnel compromise detection features that are provided for each supported role.

FR:6.118 The CKMS design **shall** specify any personnel compromise minimization features that are provided for each supported role.

FR:6.119 The CKMS design **shall** specify the CKMS compromise recovery capabilities that are provided for each supported role.

PR:6.87	PS-3	A Federal CKMS **shall** support the evaluation of each new individual before being authorized to perform any role involving FCKMS security.
PR:6.88	PS-2	A Federal CKMS **shall** perform an assessment of the potential consequences of personnel security compromises before the FKCMS initially becomes operational.

PR:6.89	AU-6 PS-1	A Federal CKMS **shall** perform an audit of its personnel security actions after a personnel security compromise is detected, and issue revisions to the FCKMS operations documentation that would reduce the likelihood of similar compromises.

PA:6.27		A Federal CKMS **should**: a) Minimize the ability of personnel accessing the FCKMS to hide any actions that could cause a security failure, b) Maintain audit records that aid in determining who or what caused the security failure, and c) Mitigate the negative consequences of a failure due to a personnel compromise.
PA:6.28		A Federal CKMS **should** perform the following after detecting an actual or probable compromise of security: a) Shut down the compromised system, b) Activate a backup facility and system with new keys or uncompromised keys, c) Notify current and potential users of the possible security compromise, and d) Revoke compromised keys.

6.8.8   Physical Security Compromise Recovery

Physical security should be used to both prevent and detect security compromises. In addition to the disclosure or destruction of keys, a physical security breach of an FCKMS module could result in compromises to the integrity of any of its internal components. A cryptographic module may be designed with adequate physical protections, but if security-related logic resides outside of the cryptographic module, then the integrity of that logic also needs protection. Techniques similar to those used by the cryptographic module should be employed. An FCKMS should support both prevention and detection mechanisms against physical compromises.

If the physical security of an FCKMS module is breached, all sensitive data within the breached area should be suspected of being compromised. The FCKMS components associated with the FCKMS module should be examined to detect any unauthorized modification or replacement. Compromised components should be repaired or replaced to prevent new keys and sensitive information from being compromised in the future.

FR:6.120 The CKMS design **shall** specify how all CKMS components and devices are protected from unauthorized physical access.

FR:6.121 The CKMS design **shall** specify how the CKMS detects unauthorized physical access.

FR:6.122 The CKMS design **shall** specify how the CKMS recovers from unauthorized physical access to components and devices other than cryptographic modules.

FR:6.123 The CKMS design **shall** specify the entities that are automatically notified if a physical security breach of any CKMS component or device is detected by the CKMS.

FR:6.124 The CKMS design **shall** specify how breached areas can be re-established to a secure state.

PR:6.90	IR-4 IR-6	A Federal CKMS **shall** support the notification of an appropriate authority of any actual or suspected physical-security compromise and initiating mitigation actions by that authority.
PR:6.91		A Federal CKMS **shall** control physical access to FCKMS devices and restrict access to only authorized entities.
PR:6.92	PE-2 (2)	For High impact-level systems, a Federal CKMS **shall** support multi-factor access control of all personnel having physical access to the FCKMS.

PA:6.29	PE-2 (2)	For Moderate impact-level systems, a Federal CKMS **should** support multi-factor access control of all personnel having physical access to the FCKMS.

PF:6.7	PE-2 (2)	For Low impact-level systems, a Federal CKMS **could** support multi-factor access control of all personnel having physical access to the FCKMS.

7   Interoperability and Transitioning

In general, interoperability is the ability of diverse systems to communicate and work together (i.e., to inter-operate). In this document, two or more entities may be considered interoperable if they are able to exchange cryptographic keys in a manner that complies with Federal standards and is considered sufficiently secure by both entities. Since this document allows for a variety of implementations to service many diverse applications, compliance with this document does not by itself guarantee interoperability. Interoperability can only be achieved by having a detailed specification and common protocols to which all communicating entities intend to comply.   These specifications and protocols may differ, depending on the applications being serviced. If no interoperability is required, then the PRs containing conditional interoperability phases are not applicable.

An FCKMS should use cryptographic algorithms and keys whose anticipated security lifetimes will span the maximum lifetime of the information being protected. If the FCKMS is intended to remain in service beyond the security lifetimes of its cryptographic algorithms, then there should be a transition strategy for migration to stronger algorithms in the future. Cryptographic algorithms should be implemented so that they can be replaced when needed. [SP 800-57 Part 1] and [SP 800-131A] specify NIST-recommended lifetimes of NIST-approved cryptographic algorithms. [SP 800-57 Part 1] provides transition guidance.

FR:7.1 The CKMS design **shall** specify how interoperability requirements across device interfaces are to be satisfied.

FR:7.2 The CKMS design **shall** specify the standards, protocols, interfaces, supporting services, commands and data formats required to interoperate with the applications it is intended to support.

FR:7.3 The CKMS design **shall** specify the standards, protocols, interfaces, supporting services, commands and data formats required to interoperate with other CKMS for which interoperability is intended.

FR:7.4 The CKMS design **shall** specify all external interfaces to applications and other CKMS.

FR:7.5 The CKMS design **shall** specify all provisions for transitions to new, interoperable, peer devices.

FR:7.6 The CKMS design **shall** specify any provisions provided for upgrading or replacing its cryptographic algorithms.

FR:7.7 The CKMS design **shall** specify how interoperability will be supported during cryptographic algorithm transition periods.

FR:7.8 The CKMS design **shall** specify its protocols for negotiating the use of cryptographic algorithms and key lengths.

The following **PR**s specify default (i.e., mandatory-to-implement) algorithms (including modes of operation, key-derivation methods, etc.) that provide FCKMS interoperability. Other **approved** algorithms may be used instead of the defaults during interactions, if previously agreed upon. Communication protocols generally include their own CKMS with selected default algorithms for interoperability; as long as the algorithms used as defaults are **approved** and are suitable for the impact level or security strength of the information being communicated, the defaults in this section are not required.

Note that the minimum security strengths to be provided by the algorithms and keys for the Low, Moderate and High impact levels are identified in **PR:2.3**, **PR:2.4** and **PR:2.5**, respectively.

PR:7.1		When interoperability is required, and a symmetric block-cipher algorithm is to be used for encryption, a Federal CKMS **shall** support AES-128 in the CBC mode as the default for Low and Moderate impact-levels, and AES-256 in the CBC mode as the default for High impact-levels, as specified in [FIPS 197] and [SP 800-38A].
PR:7.2		When interoperability is required, and a symmetric block-cipher algorithm is to be used for message authentication only[9], a Federal CKMS **shall** support AES-128 in the CMAC mode as the default for Low and Moderate impact-levels and AES-256 in the CMAC mode as the default for High impact-levels, as specified in [FIPS 197] and [SP 800-38B].
PR:7.3		When interoperability is required, and a symmetric block-cipher algorithm is to be used for authenticated encryption, a Federal CKMS **shall** support AES-128 in the GCM mode as the default for Low and Moderate impact-levels, and AES-256 in the GCM mode as the default for High impact-levels, as specified in [FIPS 197] and [SP 800-38D].
PR:7.4		When interoperability is required, and a symmetric block-cipher algorithm is to be used for key wrapping, a Federal CKMS **shall** support AES-128 in the GCM mode as the default for Low and Moderate impact-levels, and AES-256 in the GCM mode as the default for High impact-levels, as specified in [FIPS 197] and [SP 800-38D].
PR:7.5		When interoperability is required, and a hash function is to be used for a purpose that requires collision resistance[10], an FCKMS **shall** support SHA-256 as the default for Low and Moderate impact-levels, and SHA-384 as the default for High impact-levels, as specified in [FIPS 180].

[9] As opposed to authenticated encryption, which is addressed in **PR:7.3**.
[10] E.g., for the generation of a digital signature.

PR:7.6		When interoperability is required, and digital signature generation and verification is to be performed using DSA, the hash function used during signature generation and verification **shall** be selected as specified in <u>PR:7.5</u>.
PR:7.7		When interoperability is required, and digital signature generation and verification is to be performed using ECDSA, a Federal CKMS **shall** support curve P-256 as the default curve to be used for Low and Moderate impact-levels, and curve P-384 for High impact-levels. The hash function used during signature generation and verification **shall** be selected as specified in <u>PR:7.5</u>.
PR:7.8		When interoperability is required, and digital signature generation and verification is to be performed using RSA, a Federal CKMS **shall** support the RSASSA-PSS signature scheme as the default scheme. The hash function used during signature generation and verification **shall** be selected as specified in <u>PR:7.5</u>.
PR:7.9		When interoperability is required, and HMAC is to be used, a Federal CKMS **shall** support HMAC-SHA-256 as the default for Low and Moderate impact-levels, and HMAC-SHA-384 as the default for High impact-levels, as specified in <u>[FIPS 198]</u> and <u>[FIPS 180]</u>.
PR:7.10		When interoperability is required, and an interactive, finite-field DH key-agreement scheme is to be used for key establishment, a Federal CKMS **shall** support the dhEphem scheme specified in <u>[SP 800-56A]</u> as the default scheme, with the concatenation KDF as the key-derivation method. For Low and Moderate impact-level systems, the KDF **shall** use SHA-256; for High impact-level systems, the KDF **shall** use SHA-384 for the default scheme.
PR:7.11		When interoperability is required, and an interactive, elliptic-curve DH key-agreement scheme is to be used for key establishment, a Federal CKMS **shall** support the Ephemeral Unified Model scheme specified in <u>[SP 800-56A]</u> as the default scheme, with the concatenation KDF as the key-derivation method. Low and Moderate impact-level systems **shall** use curve P-256 and SHA-256 during the key-agreement transaction; High impact-level systems **shall** use curve P-384 and SHA-384.

PR:7.12		When interoperability is required, an RSA scheme is to be used for key agreement, and both participants are to use key pairs during the transaction, a Federal CKMS **shall** support the KAS2 scheme from [SP 800-56B], with the concatenation KDF employing SHA-256 as the default key-derivation method for Low and Moderate impact-levels, and SHA-384 for High impact-levels.
PR:7.13		When interoperability is required, and a one-way (e.g., store-and-forward), finite-field DH key-agreement scheme is to be used for key establishment, a Federal CKMS **shall** support the dhOneFlow scheme specified in [SP 800-56A] as the default scheme, with the concatenation KDF employing SHA-256 as the default key-derivation method for Low and Moderate impact-levels, and SHA-384 for High impact-levels.
PR:7.14		When interoperability is required, and a one-way (e.g., store-and-forward), elliptic-curve DH key-agreement scheme is to be used for key establishment, a Federal CKMS **shall** support the One-pass Diffie-Hellman scheme specified in [SP 800-56A] as the default scheme, with the concatenation KDF as the key-derivation method. Low and Moderate impact-level systems **shall** use curve P-256 and SHA-256 for the default scheme; High impact-level systems **shall** use P-384 and SHA-384.
PR:7.15		When interoperability is required, an RSA key-agreement scheme is to be used for key establishment, and only the initiator's key is to be used during the transaction, a Federal CKMS **shall** support the KAS1 scheme specified in [SP 800-56B] as the default scheme, with the concatenation KDF employing SHA-256 as the default key-derivation method for Low and Moderate impact-levels, and SHA-384 for High impact-levels.
PR:7.16		When interoperability is required, and an RSA key-transport scheme is to be used for key establishment, a Federal CKMS **shall** support the RSA-OAEP scheme specified in [SP 800-56B] as the default scheme[11].
PR:7.17		When interoperability is required, and key derivation from a pre-shared key is to be performed, a Federal CKMS **shall** support HMAC in the counter mode as specified in [SP 800-108] as the default method, using SHA-256 as the hash function for Low and Moderate impact-levels, and SHA-384 for High impact-levels.

---

[11] Note to the reader: While PKCS1 v1.5 [PKCS 1] is commonly used, it is not among the schemes that are NIST-approved in [SP 800-56B].

PR:7.18		When interoperability is required, and digital signature generation and verification is to be performed using ECDSA, a Federal CKMS **shall** support curve P-256 as the default curve and SHA-256 as the default hash function to be used for Low and Moderate impact-levels, and curve P-384 and SHA-384 for High impact-levels.
PR:7.19		When interoperability is required, and digital signature generation and verification is to be performed using RSA, a Federal CKMS **shall** support the RSASSA-PSS signature scheme as the default scheme.
PR:7.20		A CKMS **shall** use only cryptographic algorithms whose security lifetimes extend up to or beyond the anticipated lifetime of the FCKMS itself and the information that it protects, or have a transition strategy for migration to stronger algorithms and longer key lengths in the future.
PR:7.21		A Federal CKMS **shall** maintain and use transition plans that include the selection and use of cryptographic algorithm(s) and key length(s) to be used during a transition period.

| PA:7.1 | | A Federal CKMS **should** support the update or replacement of cryptographic algorithms, and do so in a manner that does not significantly impact FCKMS operations. |

| PF:7.1 | | A Federal CKMS **could** implement provisions that support transitions to new algorithms or key lengths. Such provisions include:

a) Common interfaces,
b) Common formats for keys, metadata, and associated protection mechanisms,
c) Common procedures for cryptographically associating (e.g., binding) metadata to their keys, and
d) Cryptographic algorithms that can be replaced, when needed. |

8 Security Controls

An FCKMS consists of one or more computer systems, communication services, devices, FCKMS modules, cryptographic modules, firewalls, communications and human interfaces, backup storage media, archive facilities, network security protocols, and entity identification systems. An FCKMS requires security mechanisms and management to protect FCKMS devices and components, along with the keys and metadata that they contain. These controls include physical security controls, operating system and device security controls, auditing and remote monitoring, network security controls and cryptographic module controls.

8.1 Physical Security Controls

Physical security is needed to protect the availability, reliability, and integrity of an FCKMS and to ensure the security and availability of its data-processing resources, including all key-management information and support software. Without good physical security, the FCKMS hardware and software could be modified to negate or bypass security mechanisms.

An FCKMS may include facilities that provide third-party key-management services (such as a Certification Authority, Key Distribution Center, Registration Authority, or Certificate Directory) and end-to-end communication devices (such as personal computers, personal digital assistants, smart phones, and intelligent sensing devices).

A facility is traditionally considered to be a building or room that houses equipment and support personnel in a fixed or "static" facility/environment. However, in today's world of mobile "smart" devices, the definition of a facility needs to be expanded to include the enclosure in which a mobile FCKMS module is contained (e.g., a computer laptop case, or cell phone protective cover), with some protection provided by its owner/user. A mobile device enclosure and the person carrying the enclosed device should provide protection that is similar to that available in a static facility and environment. In some instances, an FCKMS could encompass a variety of static and mobile facilities.

In a static environment, an FCKMS module could be protected by gated fences, locked doors, smart-card access-control systems, password verifiers, surveillance cameras, and guards. In a mobile environment, security will depend on the room or enclosure in which the mobile device and FCKMS module are currently operating, the person operating the mobile device, and perhaps a personal identity-verification (PIV) mechanism that is built into the device that requires an authorized owner/user to enter a special access token, secret password, and/or personal biometric characteristic (e.g., fingerprint).

FR:8.1 The CKMS design **shall** specify each of its CKMS devices and their intended purposes.

FR:8.2 The CKMS design **shall** specify the physical security controls for protecting each device containing CKMS components.

PR:8.1		A Federal CKMS **shall** support the physical protection of FCKMS modules, cryptographic modules, components, devices, and unencrypted keys and sensitive metadata.

PA:8.1	PE-3 SA-18 SC-7 SC-28	The mobile devices of a Federal CKMS **should** have physical protection against unauthorized access to the device's electronics.

8.2 Operating System and Device Security Controls

This section addresses security controls for FCKMS computer operating systems and devices. Note that an FCKMS module or device that incorporates a general-purpose operating system should also have computer security controls.

8.2.1 Operating System Security

A trusted (secure) operating system manages data to make sure that it cannot be altered, moved, or viewed except by entities having appropriate and authorized access rights. A trusted operating system should be the foundation of every modern, shared computing system, personal computer, and "smart" device. Without a trusted operating system, the security of the control programs, applications, and data on these personal devices cannot be assured. Section 8.2.1 of the Framework provides guidance on the security features that should be provided in trusted operating systems. A trusted operating system depends on a secure hardware platform running secure (operating system) software. The platform often supports two or more physically or logically separated processing capabilities in order to isolate keys, metadata, security services, and cryptographic functions according to their impact-levels, applications, users, or FCKMS Security Policies.

An FCKMS module might run on a general-purpose computer where non-validated application code is permitted. In such cases, a trusted operating system should be used to protect sensitive code and data from the non-validated code. The operating system should protect itself from all applications and should separate applications from each other. A trusted operating system is designed to provide these separations and is "trusted" to maintain a secure environment. The trusted operating system, including the hardware platform, can enforce two or more states in order to support privileged operations, such as memory management, I/O management, and secure cryptographic function calls.

Software integrity in an FCKMS must be maintained to prevent unauthorized disclosure and modification of the keys and metadata. Software integrity may be supported by using integrity mechanisms such as hash functions, message authentication codes, and digital signatures. Software integrity should be verified when the software is received from its supplier, after initial installation, upon system startup, and periodically thereafter.

Hardening is the process of eliminating a means of attack by patching vulnerabilities and turning off nonessential services. Hardening a computer involves several steps to form layers of protection. Hardening guidelines specify the procedures to be followed when hardening a system.

FR:8.3 The CKMS design **shall** specify all trusted (secure) operating system requirements (including any required operating system configurations) for each CKMS device.

FR:8.4 The CKMS design **shall** specify which of the following hardening features are enforced by the CKMS:

a) Removing all non-essential software programs and utilities from the computer;
b) Using the principle of least privilege to control access to sensitive system features and applications;
c) Using the principle of least privilege to control access to sensitive system and application files and data;
d) Limiting user accounts to those needed for legitimate operations, i.e., disabling or deleting the accounts that are no longer required;
e) Running the applications with the principle of least privilege;
f) Replacing all default passwords and keys with strong passwords and randomly generated keys, respectively;
g) Disabling or removing network services that are not required for the operation of the system;
h) Disabling or removing all other services that are not required for the operation of the system;
i) Disabling removable media, or disabling automatic run features on removable media and enabling automatic malware checks upon media introduction;
j) Disabling network ports that are not required for the system operation;
k) Enabling optional security features as appropriate; and
l) Selecting other configuration options that are secure.

FR:8.5: The CKMS design **shall** specify the BIOS protection features that ensure the proper instantiation of the operating system.

PR:8.2	CM-7 SI-3	A Federal CKMS **shall** support the following hardening procedures: a) Non-essential software is removed from computers, b) Non-essential network services are disabled, c) Non-essential FCKMS services are disabled or removed, d) Non-essential, removable data storage media or automatic run features on removable media are disabled, e) Automatic malware checks on newly attached data-storage medium are enabled, f) Non-essential network ports are disabled,

		g) The latest system patches are installed, h) The latest malware-detection software is installed, i) The appropriate file system, directory and register settings have been determined and properly configured, j) The appropriate security-relevant information to be logged has been determined and properly configured, k) The required amount of physical security has been determined and implemented, l) Default passwords and keys have been replaced with strong passwords and randomly generated keys, respectively, especially for administrator accounts, m) Unnecessary usernames and passwords have been removed, including those associated with users no longer authorized to use the system, and n) Users and access privileges have been limited to those needed for essential operations.
PR:8.3	SI-7	A Federal CKMS **shall** maintain software integrity.
PR:8.4	CM-7	A Federal CKMS **shall** protect access to sensitive keys and metadata by non-validated software.
PR:8.5	SI-6	The software for Moderate and High impact-level systems **shall** be implemented with an integrity mechanism, and the integrity of the software **shall** be verified during system startup.
PR:8.6	SC-2 SC-3	For Moderate and High impact-level systems, a Federal CKMS **shall** use trusted operating systems that separate sensitive user applications and their data from each other.
PR:8.7	AC-3 (2)	For High impact-level systems, a Federal CKMS **shall** provide multiparty control of those system functions that are considered by the FCKMS management authorities to be most critical to the security provided by the FCKMS.

PA:8.2	SI-6	The software for Low impact-level systems **should** be implemented with an integrity mechanism, and the integrity of the software **should** be verified during system startup.

PF:8.1	SC-2 SC-3	For Low impact-level systems, a Federal CKMS **could** use trusted operating systems that separate sensitive user applications from each other and from the operating system.

8.2.2 Individual FCKMS Device Security

An FCKMS may include a variety of devices. An FCKMS should be designed to protect itself from FCKMS device users and other FCKMS devices, to provide separate sessions for users and user processes, to provide fine-grained access controls on FCKMS device-level objects, to provide device-level security-event logging, and to provide entity account management.

A verification that an FCKMS device is operating correctly and securely should be established at device startup and verified periodically. The security controls incorporated into an FCKMS device could be configurable to support differences in FCKMS service-using organizations, security policies, and environments. Specific security-relevant events (such as a physical security alarm, electric power failure, unrecoverable communication errors, and human-initiated alarms) could result in different responses, depending on these differences.

FR:8.6 The CKMS design **shall** specify the security controls required for each CKMS device.

FR:8.7 The CKMS design **shall** specify the device/CKMS secure configuration requirements and guidelines that the hardening is based upon.

PR:8.8	SI-6	The correct operation of each Federal CKMS device **shall** be verified during device start-up.

PF:8.2		A Federal CKMS device **could** be manually or automatically configurable to support, comply with, and enforce new FCKMS Security Policies.

8.2.3 Malware Protection

When an FCKMS receives operating-system software, software updates and software support over electronic communication networks or via manual software distribution services, the scanning of these data items for malware may be required before installation. Scanning must be performed when the data items are untrusted, (i.e., they are received from an unauthenticated or untrustworthy source, or the data does not have sufficient cryptographic protection against undetected alteration, as determined by the impact-level of the data in the system).

Malware protection falls into the following three general categories:

a) Anti-virus software that protects an FCKMS from unwittingly installing and executing programs that perform unintended actions and may cause a security compromise,

b) Anti-spyware software that protects an FCKMS from unauthorized parties obtaining system administrator status or authorized user status, and prevents the spyware from taking on authorized device behavior, and

c) Rootkit detection and prevention software that protects FCKMS devices from rootkit malware that changes the configuration setting of the operating system in order to replace system code and hide processes and files, including the rootkit code itself, from anti-virus and anti-spyware software.

In order to be effective, malware protection should include verifying the identity of the source of the received software upon receipt, and scanning the software for malware upon initial receipt and periodically thereafter (e.g., upon reloading).

FR:8.8 The CKMS design **shall** specify the following malware protection capabilities for CKMS devices:

a) Anti-virus protection software, including the specified time periods and events that trigger anti-virus scans, software update, and virus signature database updates;

b) Anti-spyware protection software, including the specified time periods and events that trigger anti-spyware scans, software update, and virus signature updates; and

c) Rootkit detection and protection software, including the specified time periods and events that trigger rootkit detection, software update, and signature updates.

FR:8.9 The CKMS design **shall** specify the following software integrity check information for operating system and CKMS application software:

a) If software integrity is verified upon installation, indicate how the verification is performed; and

b) If software integrity is verified periodically, indicate how often the verification is performed.

PR:8.9		When untrusted software, software updates and software support may be introduced into the FCKMS, then the Federal CKMS **shall** support the following malware protection capabilities for itself and its devices: a) Anti-virus protection software, b) Anti-spyware protection software, and c) Rootkit detection and protection software.
PR:8.10		When a Federal CKMS receives untrusted software, software updates or software support, then the FCKMS **shall** perform the following before installation: a) Scan received data (including keys and metadata) when first received, and b) Verify that the updated software/firmware contains no malware before running it.
PR:8.11	RA-5 SI-4	When a Federal CKMS is allowed to receive untrusted software, software updates or software support, then the FCKMS **shall** be configured to perform (at a minimum): a) A weekly scan of installed software, b) A scan of removable media when first introduced into the CKMS,

		c) A scan of newly installed software and data files, d) A weekly update of the malware protection software, and e) A weekly update of the malware signature database.
PR:8.12	RA-5 SI-3 SI-4	When a Federal CKMS is allowed to receive untrusted software, software updates or software support, then the Federal CKMS **shall** support time-initiated and event-initiated malware scanning.

PA:8.3	SI-4	A Federal CKMS **should** support configurable, dynamic network malware monitoring.

PF:8.3	SI-4	A Federal CKMS **could** support dynamic network malware monitoring and report any identified real or potential problems to the FCKMS management personnel.

8.2.4　Auditing and Remote Monitoring

An FCKMS should monitor security-relevant events by detecting and recording these events in an audit log. The audit capability should also have the ability to detect any unusual events that should be investigated and report them to the audit administrator role as soon as possible. The audit capability and audit log must be protected from modification so that the integrity of the audit system can be assured.

Automated assessment tools, such as those specified in the Security Content Automation Protocol (SCAP) (see [SP 800-126]), should be considered for assessing the current security status and integrity of an FCKMS. Such monitoring tools could execute on the platform being monitored or on a platform dedicated to monitoring other computers.

FR:8.10 The CKMS design **shall** specify the auditable events supported and indicate whether each event is fixed or selectable.

FR:8.11 For each selectable, auditable event, the CKMS design **shall** specify the role(s) that has the capability to select the event.

FR:8.12 For each auditable event, the CKMS design **shall** specify the data to be recorded[12].

FR:8.13 The CKMS design **shall** specify what automated tools are provided to assess the correct operation and security of the CKMS.

FR:8.14 The CKMS design **shall** specify system-monitoring requirements for sensitive system files to detect and/or prevent their modification or any modification to their security attributes, such as their access control lists.

---

[12] Examples of recorded data include a unique event identifier, the date and time of the event, the subject (e.g., user, role or software process) causing the event, the success or failure of the event, and the event-specific data.

PR:8.13	AU-9	A Federal CKMS **shall** protect its audit capability and audit logs from modification and unauthorized disclosure.
PR:8.14		A Federal CKMS **shall** support the detection of attempted, but unauthorized, key and metadata access, modification, and destruction.
PR:8.15	AU-2 AU-3	A Federal CKMS **shall** support the auditing of the following security-relevant events[13] and the data to be recorded about them: a) Key generation: requestor's ID, key ID, key type, and date/time; b) Key owner registration: requestor's ID, owner's ID, key ID, authorizer's ID, and date/time; c) Key suspension: requestor's ID, key ID, reason for suspension, and date/time; d) Key reactivation after suspension: requestor's ID, key ID, justification for reactivation, and date/time; e) Key revocation: requestor's ID, key ID, reason for revocation, and date/time; f) Key destruction: requestor's ID, key ID, reason for destruction, and date/time; g) Unauthorized key and metadata modification: requestor's ID, modification requested, and date/time; h) Key and metadata recovery from backup or archived storage: requestor's ID, key-ID, key-recovery agent's ID and date/time; i) Repetitive attempts of unauthorized key access: requestor's ID, action requested, reason for rejection, and date/time. j) Key establishment: type (manual, automated), key-agreement or key-transport scheme (if appropriate), entity IDs, date/time; k) DRBG Reseed: which DRBG instance, whether requested or automatic, requestor ID (if applicable), source of entropy input, date/time.
PR:8.16	SI-4 SI-7 (+2)	For Moderate and High impact-level systems, a Federal CKMS **shall** support the monitoring of its internal modules, devices, services, functions, and files in order to detect and/or prevent their unauthorized modification, and then report the results of this monitoring to an FCKMS audit administrator.

[13] When the capability for the event is implemented.

PR:8.17	AU-2	For Moderate and High impact-level systems, a Federal CKMS **shall** support the ability for the FCKMS auditor and administrator roles to select (from an implemented set) the security-relevant events to be audited.
PR:8.18		For Moderate and High impact-level systems, a Federal CKMS **shall** support the use of SCAP to monitor the status and integrity of an FCKMS.

PA:8.4	SI-4 SI-7 (+2)	For Low impact-level systems, a Federal CKMS **should** support the monitoring of its internal components, modules, devices, services, functions, and files in order to detect and/or prevent their unauthorized modification, and then report the results of this monitoring to an FCKMS audit administrator.
PA:8.5	AU-2	For Low impact-level systems, a Federal CKMS **should** support the ability for the FCKMS auditor and administrator roles to select the security-relevant events to be audited.
PA:8.6		For Low impact-level systems, a Federal CKMS **should** support the use of SCAP to monitor the status and integrity of an FCKMS.

8.3   Network Security Control Mechanisms

Network security-control mechanisms should be used to protect computer systems and their network communications against unauthorized access and use. They should be used to detect and prevent network activities that could reduce the security of the transmitted information, especially the cryptographic keys and sensitive metadata.

Networked FCKMS devices should be protected using a combination of firewalls and intrusion detection and prevention systems as boundary-control devices. These devices should be placed in physically secure locations and used to protect FCKMS users, sensitive applications, and vulnerable network services. In order to provide defense-in-depth, boundary-control functions should also be implemented directly in FCKMS devices.

An FCKMS could be designed to be configurable or dynamic, capable of adapting to network threats based on the results of monitoring network performance, communication error detection/correction, and network overload. For example, an attempt to flood a network with repetitive or nonsense data could cause an FCKMS to not accept a data packet or connection request. An intentional and intelligent, but unauthorized, modification of network packets could result in packets being refused or a shutdown of the affected device or even the entire network.

FR:8.15 The CKMS design **shall** specify the boundary protection mechanisms employed by the CKMS.

FR:8.16 The CKMS design **shall** specify:

a) The types of firewalls used and the protocols permitted through the firewalls, including the source and destination for each type of protocol; and

b) The types of intrusion detection and prevention systems used, including their logging and security breach reaction capabilities.

FR:8.17 The CKMS design **shall** specify the methods used to protect the CKMS devices against denial of service.

FR:8.18 The CKMS design **shall** specify how each method used protects against the denial of service.

PR:8.19	AC-4 CA-3(1)	A networked Federal CKMS **shall** support the following network security-control mechanisms unless exempted by its FCKMS service-using organizations: a) Firewalls, b) Filtering routers, c) Virtual private networks (VPNs), d) Intrusion detection systems (IDS), and e) Intrusion prevention systems (IPS).
PR:8.20		A networked Federal CKMS **shall** install network security-control mechanisms in physically secure facilities.
PR:8.21	AC-3	A networked Federal CKMS **shall** allow only authorized entities to configure, initiate, activate, and disable network security-control mechanisms.
PR:8.22	IA-3	For Moderate and High impact-level systems, a Federal CKMS **shall** support the identification and authentication of each FCKMS module and device.
PR:8.23	SC-5	A Federal CKMS **shall** employ methods that minimize successful denial-of-service attacks and notify the FCKMS management personnel if any such attempted attack is detected.

PA:8.7		For Low impact-level systems, a Federal CKMS **should** support the identification and authentication of each FCKMS module and device.

8.4 Cryptographic Module Controls

A cryptographic module is a set of hardware, software and/or firmware that implements cryptographic-based security functions (e.g., cryptographic algorithms and key-establishment schemes). [FIPS 140] specifies requirements on cryptographic modules that are used by the Federal government. This Profile requires the use of FIPS 140-validated cryptographic modules (see Section 2.10).

Two primary security issues should be addressed regarding the security of the contents of cryptographic modules: the integrity of the security functions and the protection of the cryptographic keys and metadata. Since cryptographic keys are present in plaintext form for some period of time within the module, physical security measures are necessary to protect keys from unauthorized disclosure, modification, and substitution.

Each [FIPS 140] cryptographic module must be used in accordance with the cryptographic module's security policy. This detailed security policy specifies the rules for operating the cryptographic module, including the security rules that were applicable to the module and derived from [FIPS 140], and those imposed by the module developer.

FR:8.19 The CKMS design **shall** identify the cryptographic modules that it uses and their respective security policies, including:

a) The embodiment of each module (software, firmware, hardware, or hybrid),

b) The mechanisms used to protect the integrity of each module,

c) The physical and logical mechanisms used to protect each module's cryptographic keys, and

d) The third-party testing and validation that was performed on each module (including the security functions) and the protective measures employed by each module.

PR:8.24		A Federal CKMS **shall** use cryptographic modules in accordance with the security policy of that module.

8.5 Federal CKMS Security-Control Selection and Assessment Process

Federal CKMS security controls should be selected, implemented, and used in a manner that protects the FCKMS modules and cryptographic keys and metadata in accordance with [FIPS 199], [FIPS 200], [SP 800-53], and [SP 800-53A].

The process specified in the following requirements is defined and explained in [FIPS 199], [FIPS 200], [SP 800-53], and [SP800-53A]. The process will be used in Section 11 to perform a security assessment.

The results of previous device and subsystem assessments complying with the procedures of this section may be used with the approval of the System Authority without repeating the assessments.

PR:8.25		A Federal CKMS service-using organization **shall** specify the types of information to be protected by the FCKMS[14].
PR:8.26	RA-2 RA-3	A Federal CKMS **shall** comply with [FIPS 199], [FIPS 200], [SP 800-53], and [SP 800-53A] including: a) Specifying the [FIPS 199] security categories (SCs) of user applications and data, including keys and their metadata; b) Specifying the [FIPS 200] impact level of the FCKMS; c) Specifying the approved [SP 800-53] security controls protecting FCKMS users, applications, keys, and their metadata; d) Supporting the [SP 800-53] security controls, including the baseline security controls derived from the impact level of the FCKMS; e) For each security control, specifying the assurance requirements that are necessary to achieve the impact level required by the FCKMS; f) Specifying the events that would initiate an assessment of the security of the FCKMS, a reassessment of the current security controls used, and completing all corrective actions required; and g) Assessing the security controls as specified in [SP 800-53A].
PR:8.27	CA-7	The effectiveness of the Federal CKMS security controls **shall be** assessed in accordance with the continuous-monitoring guidance provided in [SP 800-53], [SP 800-53A], [SP 800-37], and [SP 800-137].
PR:8.28		Previous device and subsystem assessments that are more than one year old **shall** only be used when authorized by the system authority.

---

[14] See [SP 800-60] for guidance on commonly used information types.

9 Testing and System Assurances

Prior to the procurement of an FCKMS or FCKMS services, an FCKMS should be subjected to and pass several types of testing to ensure that it 1) conforms to its design and required standards, 2) operates according to its design specifications, 3) rejects service requests that could compromise its security, and 4) is interoperable with peer FCKMSs (if required). Various types and levels of testing should be conducted to obtain assurance that the FCKMS, including its modules and devices, performs as desired. The results of all testing should be made available to Federal government officials (perhaps as vendor-proprietary information[15]) in order to complete the evaluation processes.

PR:9.1	SA-11	The results of all testing **shall** be provided to a Federal procurement authority for review prior to the acquisition of an FCKMS.

PA:9.1	SA-11	A Federal CKMS **should** pass procurement and user acceptance testing performed by the FCKMS service provider and any third-party before procurement of the service.

9.1 CKMS and FCKMS Testing

A CKMS, including its modules and devices, should undergo tests by its vendor to verify that the CKMS performs according to its design and the CKMS Security Policy. Similarly, an FCKMS should undergo tests by the FCKMS service provider to verify that the FCKMS performs according to the FCKMS Security Policy.

FR:9.1 A CKMS design **shall** specify the non-proprietary vendor testing that was performed on the system and passed.

PR:9.2	SA-11	Prior to government acceptance of an FCKMS, the FCKMS service provider **shall** review all vendor tests that have been performed on the CKMS and its devices.
PR:9.3	SA-11	Prior to government acceptance of an FCKMS, the FCKMS service-using organization **shall** review all FCKMS service provider tests that have been performed on the FCKMS.

9.2 Third-Party Testing

An FCKMS vendor, service provider or service-using organization could initiate third-party testing of an FCKMS module or device for conformance to selected standards or to obtain specific information about the FCKMS. Third-party testing is intended to provide confidence that the designer and implementer did not overlook some flaw in their own testing procedures or error in the testing results. For example, the National Institute of Standards and Technology has established several programs for validating conformance

---

[15] Proprietary test results must be marked appropriately, packaged separately, and handled securely.

to its cryptographic standards and recommendations, including the Cryptographic Module Validation Program (CMVP) and the Cryptographic Algorithm Validation Program (CAVP). Non-cryptographic software and hardware could be validated using the Common Criteria Standard ([ISO 15408 Parts 1- 3] by the National Information Assurance Partnership (NIAP)). These validations produce a high level of assurance regarding specific characteristics of a product or service.

FR:9.2 The CKMS design **shall** specify all third-party testing programs that have been passed to date by the CKMS or its devices.

PR:9.4	SA-4 SA-11 SC-13	Cryptographic modules to be incorporated into a Federal CKMS **shall** be validated within NIST's Cryptographic Module Validation Program (CMVP).
PR:9.5	SA-4 SA-11 SC-13	All NIST-**approved** cryptographic algorithms used by Federal CKMS cryptographic modules **shall** pass all the appropriate CAVP tests.

PA:9.2	SA-11	Non-cryptographic software and hardware used within a Federal CKMS **should** be validated using the Common Criteria Standard ([ISO 15408 Parts 1- 3], National Information Assurance Partnership (NIAP)).
PA:9.3		All Federal CKMS modules and devices **should** be tested by a third-party, and the test results **should** be provided to the appropriate FCKMS procurement authorities for review.

9.3 Interoperability Testing

Interoperability testing, in its most general form, merely tests that two or more devices can be interconnected and operate with one another. This means that the data exchanged between the devices must be in a format that each device can process. Interoperable devices may be interconnected to form a system, and interoperable systems may be interconnected to form a network. Note that this type of testing does not necessarily test the internal functioning of the individual device. If a device performs a unique function, interoperability testing may not verify that function.

FR:9.3 If a CKMS claims interoperability with another system, then the CKMS design **shall** specify the tests that have been performed and passed that verify the claim.

FR:9.4 If a CKMS claims interoperability with another system, then the CKMS design **shall** specify any configuration settings that are required for interoperability.

PR:9.6		If an FCKMS, FCKMS module, or FCKMS device claims interoperability with a reference implementation, then the FCKMS, FCKMS module or FCKMS device **shall** be tested and validated against the reference implementation.

9.4 Self-Testing

An FCKMS module or device could be designed, implemented, and operate correctly when first deployed, but then fail some time later. A Federal CKMS must use modules and devices that test themselves for functionality, integrity and security.

FR:9.5 The CKMS design **shall** specify all self-tests created and implemented by the designer and the corresponding CKMS functions whose correct operation they verify.

PR:9.7		A Federal CKMS **shall** perform initial and periodic self-tests that verify the continued correctness of the system.
PR:9.8	SI-6 SI-7	For Moderate and High impact-level systems, a Federal CKMS **shall** verify its software integrity after initial installation, update installation, system power-on, and then daily thereafter.

PA:9.4	SI-6 SI-7	For Low impact-level systems, a Federal CKMS **should** verify its software integrity after initial installation, update installation, system power-on, and then daily thereafter.

9.5 Scalability Testing

Scalability is a characteristic of a system, network, or process to perform increasing amounts of work correctly. Scalability testing involves testing a device or system to learn how it reacts when the number of transactions to be processed or participants to be serviced properly during a given period of time increases dramatically. Scalability testing can be used to stress devices and systems so that overload problems are detected and mitigated before encountering these problems during operational use.

FR:9.6 The CKMS design **shall** specify all scalability analysis and testing performed on the system to date.

PR:9.9		A Federal CKMS **shall** be subjected to scalability tests.

9.6 Functional and Security Testing

Functional testing is used to verify that an implementation performs correctly. For example, a functional test could verify that an implemented encryption algorithm produces the correct ciphertext. Functional testing includes performing and passing the types of tests specified in Sections 9.2 - 9.5 or obtaining evidence that these tests have been performed and produced acceptable results.

Security testing is used to verify that an implementation operates securely. For example, a security test could verify that fluctuations in power consumption or other outside influences will not compromise the key of a correctly operating device. Thus, a cryptographic algorithm implementation may be required to pass both functional testing and security testing.

Penetration testing is a specific type of security testing in which a team of testing experts attacks one or more of a system's computers or devices to defeat its security. Prior to penetration testing, the FCKMS is analyzed for potential vulnerabilities that could be exploited by the penetration team. Such vulnerabilities could result from an incomplete CKMS design, an improper FCKMS configuration, hardware or software flaws, or operational weaknesses in key-management services or technical countermeasures. The scope of penetration testing should include FCKMS hardware, software, personnel procedures, facilities, and environmental services. Any findings of, and conclusions reached by, the penetration testing team should be addressed before initial deployment of the FCKMS.

Note that individual FCKMS product/device penetration testing could be conducted as part of an FCKMS security assessment (see Section 11).

FR:9.7 The CKMS design **shall** specify the functional and security testing that was performed on the system and the results of the tests.

PR:9.10	SA-11	A Federal CKMS **shall** pass functional and security testing before its initial operation.
PR:9.11		Functional testing **shall** include performing and passing the following types of tests or obtaining evidence that the tests were performed and produced acceptable results: a) Third-party testing, where available, b) Interoperability testing, c) Self testing, and d) Scalability testing.
PR:9.12	CA-8 SA-11	For High impact-level systems, a Federal FCKMS **shall** pass penetration testing before initial operation, and before resuming operations after major changes.
PR:9.13		A Federal CKMS **shall** conduct functional and security testing annually or in accordance with a Service Level Agreement (SLA), and continue operation only if the tests are passed or the system supports operation in a degraded mode.

PA:9.5	CA-8 SA-11	For Low and Moderate impact-level systems, a Federal FCKMS **should** pass penetration testing before initial operation, and before resuming operations after major changes.

SP 800-152   A Profile for U.S. Federal CKMS

PF:9.1		The functional and security testing performed on a Federal CKMS **could** be automated.

9.7   Environmental Testing

CKMS designers often assume a particular environment (e.g., temperature range and voltage range) in which a proposed CKMS product will operate. The CKMS is then designed, built and tested for use within that environment. If the products are used in a different environment, secure operation could be lost. A CKMS being considered for procurement for Moderate and High impact-level systems should either employ environmental failure protection mechanisms or pass environmental testing before becoming operational. Note that at security level 4, [FIPS 140] requires environmental failure testing of cryptographic modules.

FR:9.8 The CKMS design **shall** specify the environmental conditions in which the CKMS is designed to be used.

FR:9.9 The CKMS design **shall** specify the conditions that are required for its secure operation.

FR:9.10 The CKMS design **shall** specify the results of environmental testing that was performed on the CKMS devices, including the results of all tests stressing the devices beyond the conditions for which they were designed.

PA:9.6		For Moderate and High impact-level systems, Federal CKMS modules **should** either employ environmental failure protection mechanisms or pass environmental testing before becoming operational.

9.8   Ease-of-Use Testing

An FCKMS should be easy to use, manage, and maintain. In order to evaluate ease-of-use, a panel of people having different expertise and experience typically creates evaluation criteria, and selects and monitors user-device-interface ease-of-use evaluation tests that are performed by a test group of users.

An FCKMS could support a demonstration of correct FCKMS usage, and could be designed to adapt to a user's experience and abilities. An FCKMS must automatically detect incorrect user input, including the length, format and range of the expected input (see PR:3.2 in Section 3.4.2).

PR:9.14		Federal CKMS interfaces **shall** be tested and approved by the service provider and the service using organization for ease-of-use (including the features designed to detect and/or mitigate incorrect user input) prior to procurement and when any human-to-FCKMS interface changes are made.

98

PF:9.2		A Federal CKMS **could** support automated demonstrations of its capabilities and ease of operation.
PF:9.3		A Federal CKMS **could** adapt to a user's experience and abilities.
PF:9.4		A Federal CKMS **could** be tested for ease-of-use by a third-party prior to procurement.

9.9 Development, Delivery, and Maintenance Assurances

The secure development, delivery, and maintenance of CKMS products can play a significant role in the security of the CKMS. The following areas should be considered:

a) Configuration management,

b) Secure delivery,

c) Development and maintenance environmental security, and

d) Flaw remediation.

Each of these areas is described in the following subsections.

9.9.1 Configuration Management

An FCKMS should incorporate products that are developed and maintained under an appropriate configuration management system in order to ensure that security is not reduced, and functional flaws are not introduced due to unauthorized or unintentional changes to the products.

FR:9.11 The CKMS design **shall** specify:

a) The devices (including their source code, documentation, build scripts, executable code, firmware, hardware design specification, documentation, and test code) to be kept under configuration control.

b) The protection requirements (e.g., formal authorizations and proper record keeping) to ensure that only authorized changes are made to the components and devices under configuration control.

PR:9.15	CM-2 CM-3 CM-9 SA-10	A Federal CKMS **shall** be under configuration management during design, implementation, procurement, installation, configuration, operation, maintenance, and final destruction.
PR:9.16		The Federal CKMS configuration management system **shall** maintain records of the make, model, version, and identification number of each FCKMS module and device.

9.9.2 Secure Delivery

When the computers, software, modules, and devices that are to be used in an FCKMS are delivered, assurance of secure delivery (i.e. that the products received are the exact products that were ordered) is required.

FR:9.12 The CKMS design **shall** specify secure delivery requirements for the products used in the CKMS, including:

a) Protection requirements to ensure that the product has not been tampered with during the delivery process or that tampering is detected,

b) Protection requirements to ensure that the product has not been replaced during the delivery process or that replacement is detected,

c) Protection requirements to ensure that an unrequested delivery is detected, and

d) Protection requirements to ensure that the product delivery is not suppressed or delayed and that suppression or delay is detected.

PR:9.17	SA-12 (+10)	A Federal CKMS **shall** verify that: a) The delivered product has not been tampered with during the delivery process, b) The product has not been replaced during the delivery process, c) Delivered but unauthorized items are not used, and d) Product delivery is not suppressed or delayed.
PR:9.18	SA-12	A Federal CKMS **shall** support the notification of FCKMS management personnel when: a) Any modification or replacement of the expected delivery item is detected, b) Any delay or cancellation of product delivery is detected, or c) Any unauthorized delivery is received.

9.9.3 Development and Maintenance Environmental Security

The CKMS development and FCKMS maintenance environments must be protected against physical, technical, and personnel threats. Tools such as compilers, software loaders, and text editors should not be automatically trusted.

FR:9.13 The CKMS design **shall** specify the security requirements for the development and maintenance environments of the CKMS, including:

a) Physical security requirements,

b) Personnel security requirements, such as clearances and background checks for developers, testers, and maintainers,

c) Procedural security, such as multiparty control and separation of duties,

d) Computer security controls to protect the development and maintenance environment and to provide access control to permit authorized user access,

e) Network security controls to protect the development and maintenance environment from hacking attempts,

f) Cryptographic security control to protect the integrity of software and its control data under development, and

g) The means used to ensure that the tools (e.g., editors, compiler, software linkers, loaders, etc.) are trustworthy and are not sources of malware.

PR:9.19		A Federal CKMS service-providing organization **shall** verify that the CKMS designer, developer, and implementer followed the claimed procedures for the development and maintenance environment documented in **FR:9.13**.
PR:9.20	MA-1 SA-18	A Federal CKMS **shall** protect against physical, technical, and personnel threats during FCKMS maintenance activities.

9.9.4   Flaw Remediation Capabilities

The detection, reporting, and correction of FCKMS flaws must be done in an expeditious and secure manner. Users should report potential and detected flaws to the FCKMS management. An FCKMS that employs automated flaw-detection techniques is highly desirable because it can continuously monitor its own security status, report potential problems to an authorized person fulfilling an appropriate FCKMS role, and minimize reliance on human monitoring of events that occur infrequently.

FR:9.14 The CKMS design **shall** specify the CKMS capabilities for detecting system flaws, including:

a) Known-answer tests,

b) Error detection codes,

c) Anomaly diagnostics, and

d) Functional Testing.

FR:9.15 The CKMS design **shall** specify the CKMS capability for reporting flaws, including: the capability to produce status report messages with confidentiality, integrity and source authentication protections, and to detect unauthorized delays.

FR:9.16 The CKMS design **shall** specify the CKMS capability for analyzing flaws and creating/obtaining fixes for likely or commonly known flaws.

FR:9.17 The CKMS design **shall** specify its capability to transmit fixes with confidentiality, integrity and source authentication protections and to detect unauthorized delays.

FR:9.18 The CKMS design **shall** specify its capability for implementing fixes in a timely manner.

PR:9.21	SA-11 SI-2	A Federal CKMS **shall** support the detection, reporting, and timely correction of security-compromising flaws by supporting one or more methods for: a) Users to report flaws to the FCKMS management, b) Confidentiality and integrity protection of the flaw report, c) Submitting the flaw report to the CKMS designer, and d) Determining the appropriate action to be taken about FCKMS information affected by the flaw.

PF:9.5		A Federal CKMS **could** support automated flaw-detection and reporting of potential security problems to FCKMS management personnel.

10 Disaster Recovery

An FCKMS failure could hamper or prevent access to an organization's information. For example, the inability to decipher information because the key is destroyed or unrecoverable will prevent access to the plaintext data because the information cannot be decrypted. This section describes how operational continuity can be achieved in the event of device failures or the corruption of keys and metadata.

Disaster recovery requires having procedures and sufficient backup capability to recover from facility damage, utility service outages, communication and computation outages, hardware and software failures, and other failures that result in the corruption of keys and metadata.

Several of the PRs and PAs in this section include a specific time frame for recovery. Alternatively, recovery could be in accordance with a Service Level Agreement (SLA) between a service provider and a service-using organization; the SLA is a service contract where the service is formally defined. The specific times provided in the PRs and PAs can be used to determine whether recovery times specified in the SLA are reasonable for the FCKMS and its associated applications. Note that the required recovery times may not be the same for all applications, so the time frames provided in an SLA can be customized.

PR:10.1	CP-6 CP-9 (6)	A Federal CKMS **shall** be installed and operated with sufficient backup capability to ensure operational continuity.

PA:10.1	CP-2 (3, 4)	A Federal CKMS **should** have procedures and sufficient backup capability to recover to a secure state following a detected failure within 24 hours or a time period specified in a Service Level Agreement (SLA).

PF:10.1	CP-2 (3, 4)	A Federal CKMS **could** have procedures and sufficient backup capability to recover to a secure state within one hour following a detected failure.

10.1 Facility Damage

FCKMS components should be located in physically secure and environmentally protected facilities. Facilities may be either fixed or mobile.

For an FCKMS module in a fixed facility, wind, water and fire damage are common risks. For mobile facilities, risks also include physical damage, accidental loss, theft, destruction, and a higher probability of use by unauthorized entities than is the case for a fixed facility. For mobile devices that contain FCKMS capabilities, the enclosure is considered to be the facility (see Section 8.1) and should have physical protection against unauthorized access to the device's electronics. Mobile devices could be provided with waterproof containers and owner-identity verification mechanisms (e.g., fingerprint scanner and verifier). However, low-cost mobile devices often do not have the built-in tamper protection features of a fixed device. Therefore, the owner who carries and uses a secure mobile device is responsible for protecting it against physical damage, loss, and unauthorized use.

Mobile devices have the advantage that they may be easily replaced when they are damaged.

Whether an FCKMS module is operated in a fixed or mobile facility, a backup facility or capability should be available, and the FCKMS should support reporting and recovery procedures in the event of damage to a primary FCKMS facility. FCKMS facilities should be designed, implemented, and operated in a manner commensurate with the value and sensitivity of the information being protected.

When a facility is damaged, secret and private keys and keys associated with sensitive metadata that could have been disclosed should be immediately placed on Compromised Key Lists or Certificate Revocation Lists and replaced.

FR:10.1 The CKMS design **shall** specify the required environmental, fire, and physical access control protection mechanisms and procedures for recovery from damage to the primary and all backup facilities.

PR:10.2	PE-2 PE-3 PE-5 PE-6 PE-8 PE-13 PE-14 PE-15 PE-16 PE-18 PE-19	For High impact-level systems, the devices of a Federal CKMS **shall** be located in physically secure and environmentally protected facilities.
PR:10.3	CP-2 CP-6 CP-7 CP-9 (+3, 6)	For Moderate and High impact-level systems, the fixed facilities of a Federal CKMS **shall** have backup facilities and capabilities so that the FCKMS can resume normal operations within twelve hours of a failure of the primary facility or in accordance with a Service Level Agreement.
PR:10.4	CP-2 CP-8 CP-10	A Federal CKMS **shall** support recovery procedures in the event of the damage or loss of an FCKMS capability.
PR:10.5	PE-3	A Federal CKMS **shall** be operated in facilities that provide levels of protection and availability that are commensurate with the impact-level associated with the information being protected.

PR:10.6		When a primary facility is damaged, and a backup facility is available, a Federal CKMS **shall** activate its backup facility and place keys that have been, or could have been, compromised on Compromised Key or Certificate Revocation Lists and replace those keys, if required for operational continuity.
PR:10.7		A Federal CKMS **shall** be tested annually or in accordance with a Service Level Agreement to determine that facility-damage detection and recovery mechanisms and procedures work as required.
PR:10.8		The procedures for maintaining and testing the environmental, physical, and disaster recovery capabilities of a Federal CKMS **shall** be evaluated every five years or in accordance with a Service Level Agreement and upgraded as needed.
PR:10.9		Damaged or lost FCKMS devices **shall** be reported to FCKMS management personnel.

PA:10.2	PE-2 PE-3 PE-5 PE-6 PE-8 PE-13 PE-14 PE-15 PE-16 PE-18 PE-19	For Low and Moderate impact-level systems, the devices of a Federal CKMS **should** be located in physically secure and environmentally protected facilities.
PA:10.3		A Federal CKMS component in a fixed facility **should** be tested every six months or in accordance with a Service Level Agreement to verify that adequate environmental, fire, and physical protection is available.
PA:10.4	CP-2 CP-6 CP-7 CP-9 (+3, 6)	For Low impact-level systems, the fixed facilities of a Federal CKMS **should** have backup facilities and capabilities so that the FCKMS can resume normal operations within forty-eight hours of a failure of the primary facility or in accordance with a Service Level Agreement.
PA:10.5		A Federal CKMS mobile facility **should** have one or more backup facilities available to replace the facility in the event of loss or destruction.

PF:10.2		A Federal CKMS **could** have one or more archive facilities for long-term storage of keys and metadata.

10.2 Utility Service Outage

An FCKMS module in a fixed facility requires reliable utility services (e.g., electrical power) for assuring its availability. Other required services could include water, sewer, air conditioning, heat, and clean air. Adequate utility services in all primary and backup fixed facilities must be available to support all electronic devices, human safety and comfort during normal operations and emergencies, and should be provided to all primary and backup facilities.

Mobile devices with FCKMS capabilities will require battery chargers and may require backup batteries.

Backup systems should have utility services that are independent from those of the primary system. For example, a surge from a power-line lightning strike could cause both the primary system and its backup to fail if they are both served by the same power line.

FR:10.2 The CKMS design **shall** specify the minimum, as well as recommended electrical, water, sanitary, heating, cooling, and air filtering requirements for the primary and all backup facilities.

PR:10.10	PE-9 (1) PE-11 PE-12	A Federal CKMS **shall** be provided with sufficient utility services to support all primary and backup fixed facilities during both normal operation and emergencies.
PR:10.11		A Federal CKMS **shall** conform to applicable Federal and industry standards for utility assurance and satisfy the CKMS design requirements for utility services for all primary, backup, and archive facilities.
PR:10.12	CP-8 (3)	For High impact-level systems, the utility service for a backup system of a Federal CKMS **shall** be independent from that of the primary system.

PA:10.6	CP-8 (3)	For Low and Moderate impact-level systems, the utility service for a backup system of a Federal CKMS **should** be independent from that of the primary system.

10.3 Communication and Computation Outage

An FCKMS needs sufficient communication and computation capabilities to perform its required functions and to provide the key-management services that are required by its users. Backup communication and computation capabilities should be provided by an FCKMS in the event of system failure. The ability to access alternative communication services is highly desirable in the event of a communication-service failure.

FR:10.3 The CKMS design **shall** specify the communications and computation redundancy present in the design and required to be available during operation in order to assure continued operation of services commensurate with the anticipated needs of users, enterprises, and CKMS applications.

PR:10.13	CP-2 CP-8 (3) CP-9 (6) CP-11	When high reliability and availability of the FCKMS services is required, a Federal CKMS **shall** have backup communications, computation, and electrical services available that can be activated as needed.
PR:10.14	CP-2 (+3, 4) CP-7 CP-8 (+1, 2, 3)	A Federal CKMS **shall** have the computation and communication redundancy needed to recover from computation or communication failures within twelve hours or in a time period specified within a Service-Level Agreement (SLA).

PF:10.3	CP-7 (+3, 4)	A Federal CKMS **could** support automatic switching to backup computation and communication services within fifteen minutes of a detected utility-service outage.

10.4 FCKMS Hardware Failure

Since an FCKMS is critical for the secure operation of the information-management system that it supports, it is desirable to minimize the impact of hardware failures of FCKMS components and devices. Replacement parts should be available for critical devices, or complete system redundancy should be available to obtain assurance that the operational impact of a hardware failure is minimal, i.e., limited to reduced performance and response time. Some backup systems maintain real-time synchronization with the primary system. Such systems are capable of immediately taking over the responsibilities of the primary system. Other systems synchronize periodically and have a catch-up procedure to bring the backup system up to the state that the primary system had just before the failure occurred.

It is essential that backup systems have as much independence from the primary system as possible so that a failure to the primary system does not also result in the same failure to the backup. Multiple backup systems could be used to provide error-detection capabilities.

Redundant FCKMS devices can be used to provide error-detection and correction capabilities. Two FCKMS devices performing the same services can detect discrepancies in the results of a key-management function; three systems, all performing the same function, can detect a failure in one system and correct a single failure using the results of the other two devices, assuming that the results are the same. Since redundancy multiplies the cost of providing key-management services, FCKMS service-providing organizations should attempt to find an optimum trade-off between redundancy and cost.

FR:10.4 The CKMS design **shall** specify the strategy for backup and recovery from failures of hardware components and devices.

PR:10.15	CP-9 (+2)	A Federal CKMS **shall** perform initial and periodic tests of backup and recovery capabilities of its critical FCKMS modules and devices.
PR:10.16		A Federal CKMS **shall** test the backup and recovery of services requiring high availability at least annually or in accordance with a Service Level Agreement.
PR:10.17		A Federal CKMS **shall** perform tests of security-critical hardware monthly or in accordance with a Service Level Agreement.
PR:10.18		A Federal CKMS **shall** repair or replace failed critical hardware and be returned to operational status within 24 hours of a failure or in accordance with a Service Level Agreement.

PF:10.4		A Federal CKMS **could** repair or replace failed hardware and be returned to operational status within one hour of a failure when high availability is required.
PF:10.5		A Federal CKMS **could** automatically verify the operational readiness of its backup services.

10.5 System Software Failure

Software errors can have security results ranging from minor problems to catastrophic failures. Corrupted software must be detected using integrity tests and replaced as soon as possible if errors are found; such tests include the computation of cryptographic error-detection codes (e.g., message authentication codes and digital signatures) and other values determined by the code itself (i.e., known answers) that are periodically recomputed on the currently used software for comparison with the originally computed values to verify that the software is still correct. If an error is detected, an error state should be entered, and an error report should be sent to the FCKMS management.

When a primary FCKMS facility is restored from backup, the most recent information since the last secure state was backed up could be missing, since it was not included in the backup. Full secure-state FCKMS backups should be performed on a regular basis, and the latest FCKMS secure state should be reloaded into a repaired-and-ready FCKMS component or device upon the detection of a software failure.

Note that when a primary FCKMS facility is restored from backup, the most recent information since the last secure state was backed up could be missing, since it may have not been included in the backup.

FR:10.5 The CKMS design **shall** specify all techniques provided by the CKMS to verify the correctness of the system software.

FR:10.6 The CKMS design **shall** specify all techniques provided by the CKMS to detect alterations or garbles to the software once it is loaded into memory.

FR:10.7 The CKMS design **shall** specify the strategy for backup and recovery from a major software failure.

PR:10.19	SA-4	A Federal CKMS **shall** use software that has passed pre-operational self-tests that verify its integrity before becoming operational.
PR:10.20		A Federal CKMS **shall** perform backups of its software only after the current software passes its integrity self-tests.
PR:10.21		A Federal CKMS **shall** perform software and critical-data backups daily or in accordance with a Service-Level Agreement.
PR:10.22		A Federal CKMS **shall** reload its software from the latest FCKMS secure-state backup or the original code itself after a software failure is detected or suspected.
PR:10.23		A Federal CKMS **shall** perform full secure-state backups at least weekly or in accordance with a Service Level Agreement.
PR:10.24		A Federal CKMS **shall** ensure that all software errors are analyzed and repaired before the system is returned to a fully operational state.

PF:10.6		A Federal CKMS **could** automatically verify correct operation of the FCKMS software and hardware by randomly performing supported key-management functions simultaneously in the primary and backup facilities and verifying that the results are identical.

10.6 Cryptographic Module Failure

Cryptographic modules should have built-in tests that are adequate to detect hardware, software, or firmware failures. [FIPS-140]-validated modules perform pre-operational, conditional, and periodic self-tests. If a failure is detected, the module enters an error state that outputs an error indicator and determines if the error is a non-recoverable type (i.e. one that requires service, repair, or replacement) or a recoverable type (i.e., one that requires initialization or resetting). If the error is recoverable, the module should be rebooted and pass all power-up self-tests before performing normal processing. If the error recurs after repeated attempts to reboot, then the module should be replaced.

FR:10.8 The CKMS design **shall** specify what self-tests are used by each cryptographic module to detect errors and verify the integrity of the module.

FR:10.9 The CKMS design **shall** specify how each cryptographic module responds to detected errors.

FR:10.10 The CKMS design **shall** specify its strategy for the repair or replacement of failed cryptographic modules.

PF:10.7		A Federal CKMS **could** automatically switch FCKMS processing to a backup cryptographic module upon detection or suspicion of a cryptographic module failure.

10.7 Corruption and Loss of Keys and Metadata

Cryptographic keys and metadata can be corrupted or lost during transmission or in storage. If a lost key, a corrupted key, or a key with corrupted metadata, has been used to protect data, the security consequences should be evaluated, since a loss or compromise of sensitive data could result.

Lost keys must be revoked, but may be recovered from reliable storage if used only for processing already-protected information, and the risk of doing so is acceptable. Users must be aware that the key may have been compromised, and the protected data is suspect.

Corrupted keys and metadata should be either replaced or recovered from reliable storage (e.g., backup) as soon as the corruption is detected if needed for continued operation.

FR:10.11 The CKMS design **shall** specify its procedures for backing-up and archiving cryptographic keys and their metadata.

FR:10.1210.5 The CKMS design **shall** specify its procedures for restoring or replacing corrupted keys and metadata that have been stored or transmitted.

PR:10.25		A Federal CKMS **shall** support: a) Periodically checking for lost or corrupted keys and/or metadata, b) Reporting lost or corrupted keys and/or metadata to the FCKMS management and affected entities, c) Preventing the use of lost or corrupted keys and/or metadata for applying cryptographic protection, and d) Replacing lost or corrupted keys and/or metadata.
PR:10.26		A Federal CKMS **shall** revoke lost keys as soon as detected or suspected.

PR:10.27		If lost keys are recovered, they **shall** be recovered from reliable storage and used only for processing already-protected information if the risk of such use is acceptable.

PA:10.7		A Federal CKMS **should** evaluate the potential consequences of having used a lost or corrupted key and/or metadata.
PA:10.8		A Federal CKMS **should** revoke corrupted keys as soon as detected.
PA:10.9		If corrupted keys are required for continued operation, they **should** be recovered from reliable storage or replaced.

PF:10.8		A Federal CKMS **could** automatically report corrupted keys and metadata to all potentially affected entities, and initiate recovery and replacement procedures.

11 Security Assessment

Security should be assessed periodically throughout the entire lifetime of a Federal CKMS. This section describes assessments that should be made prior to its initial operation, during periodic (e.g., annual) reviews, and after major changes. For additional information on security assessment practices and controls, see [SP 800-37], [SP 800-53], [SP 800-53A], and [SP 800-115].

A team of experienced people should perform a security assessment with expertise in several areas that are selected, based on the type of assessment being conducted. A security-assessment team should consist of individuals who possess expertise in these areas and in the planned security assessment topic.

PA:11.1		A Federal CKMS **should** be subjected to security assessments by a team of people that collectively have experience and expertise in: a) Computer security, b) Cryptography, c) Cryptographic protocols, d) Distributed system design, e) Human usability/accessibility requirements, f) Key management, g) Network security, h) Information security, i) Secure information system laws, regulations and standards, j) Secure system design, and k) Security assessments.

11.1 Full Security Assessment

Following installation, but prior to its initial operation, the security of an FCKMS should be fully assessed.

FR:11.1 The CKMS design **shall** specify the necessary assurance activities to be undertaken prior to or in conjunction with a full CKMS security assessment.

FR:11.2 The CKMS design **shall** specify the circumstances under which a full security assessment is to be repeated.

PR:11.1	CA-1 CA-2 SA-11	A Federal CKMS **shall** undergo a full security assessment including the following: a) A review of the goals of the implemented system, along with a written justification as to how the FCKMS supports the goals; b) An architectural review;

| | | c) A review of the results of security tests conducted by third-party testing organizations;
d) Functional and security testing;
e) Penetration testing (when required);
f) An assessment to ensure that the FCKMS supports the FCKMS security policies of its service-using organizations;
g) An assessment of the FCKMS security controls as described and required in Section 8.5; and
h) An overall assessment of the security of the FCKMS. |
| PR:11.2 | CA-2 | A Federal CKMS **shall** undergo and pass a full security assessment under the following circumstances:

a) Before initial operation,
b) After a significant change to any policy affecting the security of the FCKMS,
c) After major system changes, and
d) Immediately after the occurrence or suspected occurrence of a compromise. |

| PA:11.2 | | A Federal CKMS **should** support all interfaces that are needed for testing by a security-assessment team. |

11.1.1 Review of Third-Party Testing and Verification of Test Results

Even though no formal validation programs for the security of an entire FCKMS currently exist, certain programs have been established to test parts of the FCKMS, including:

a) NIST's Cryptographic Algorithm Validation Program (CAVP), which tests NIST-approved cryptographic algorithms against their specifications,

b) NIST's Cryptographic Module Validation Program (CMVP), which tests cryptographic modules against the requirements in [FIPS 140], and

c) The National Information Assurance Partnership (NIAP), which tests non-cryptographic software and hardware against the Common Criteria Standard (see [ISO 15408 Parts 1- 3]).

Even though these programs do not guarantee security, they can significantly increase confidence in the security and integrity of an FCKMS.

FR:11.3 The CKMS design **shall** specify all validation programs under which any of the CKMS devices have been validated.

FR:11.4 The CKMS design **shall** specify all validation certificate numbers for its validated devices.

PR:11.3		During a full security assessment, the assessment team for a Federal CKMS **shall** verify that NIST-approved cryptographic algorithms are supported in the FCKMS and have been validated under the NIST Cryptographic Algorithm Validation Program (CAVP).
PR:11.4		During a full security assessment, the assessment team for a Federal CKMS **shall** verify that all cryptographic modules used by the FCKMS have been validated for conformance to FIPS 140 under the NIST Cryptographic Module Validation Program (CMVP).

PA:11.3		During a full security assessment, the assessment team for a Federal CKMS **should** verify that non-cryptographic software and hardware (e.g. operating systems, DBMS, or firewalls) used in or by the FCKMS have been validated using the Common Criteria Standard (see [ISO 15408 Parts 1- 3]) under the National Information Assurance Partnership (NIAP)

11.1.2 Architectural Review of System Design

An architectural review is an examination of a system's security architecture by a qualified team of experts to determine that the basic design is consistent with its security goals. This review is required in Section 11.1 for all FCKMS(s).

FR:11.5 The CKMS design **shall** specify whether an architectural review is required as part of the full security assessment.

FR:11.6 If an architectural review is required, then the CKMS design **shall** specify the skill set required by the architectural review team.

PR:11.5		During an architectural review, the assessment team for a Federal CKMS **shall** have access to all CKMS design information, third-party-validation information, and the available results of FCKMS/CKMS testing.

PA:11.4		When penetration testing is to be performed on a Federal CKMS, the penetration-testing scenarios **should** be determined by the architectural review team.
PA:11.5	SA-4	A Federal CKMS using-organization **should** analyze the results of the architectural review before procuring an FCKMS.

11.1.3 Functional and Security Testing

Functional and security testing of an FCKMS should be performed prior to initial deployment, during subsequent periodic security reviews, and during incremental security assessments. Functional and security tests could be performed by the CKMS developer, CKMS implementer, the FCKMS service provider, or a trusted third-party. These tests could also be performed, or the results reviewed, by an FCKMS-using organization.

Functional testing should include usability tests for users whose knowledge and experience with an FCKMS range from novice to expert. An FCKMS is considered to be "user-friendly" when it can be easily used by novice users, or when the services are automatically provided and controlled by an FCKMS that is "transparent" to the user.

FR:11.7 The CKMS design **shall** specify all required functional and security testing of the CKMS.

FR:11.8 The CKMS design **shall** report the results of all functional and security tests performed to date.

PR:11.6	SA-11	A Federal CKMS **shall** undergo functional and security testing, including ease-of-use tests before initial operation.

PF:11.1		A Federal CKMS **could** automatically test the security and functionality of all of its services that are intended to support and interact with other security domains and report the results to all participating security domain administrators.

11.1.4 Penetration Testing

Penetration tests are used to determine the extent to which a system resists active attempts to compromise its security. This type of testing requires security experts who are knowledgeable about typical system weaknesses and attacks against them, and who can create new or unsuspected attack methods. The penetration-testing team for an FCKMS should include some individuals who are not part of the CKMS design or implementation team and who do not have preconceived notions about its security.

FR:11.9 The CKMS design **shall** specify the results of any completed penetration testing performed to date.

PR:11.7	CA-8	Penetration testing **shall** be performed on High impact-level Federal CKMSs.
PR:11.8	CA-8 (+1) SA-11 (5)	When penetration testing is to be performed on a Federal CKMS, the penetration testing team **shall** include individuals who did not assist in the CKMS design or implementation.

PA:11.6		A penetration-testing team **should** include individuals with experience in computer and communication systems design and testing, software testing, vulnerability analysis, and security threat analysis.
PA:11.7	SA-11 (5)	When penetration testing has been performed on a Federal CKMS, the system **should** undergo penetration testing at least every two years or in accordance with a Service Level Agreement.

11.2 Periodic Security Review

FCKMS system controls, physical controls, procedural controls and personnel controls should be reviewed periodically to ensure that these controls are in place and operational. Issues identified from the review should be addressed. In addition, periodic functional and security testing should be performed (see Section 9.6).

FR:11.10 The CKMS design **shall** specify the periodicity of security reviews.

FR:11.11 The CKMS design **shall** specify the scope of the security review in terms of the CKMS devices.

FR:11.12 The CKMS design **shall** specify the scope of the periodic security review in terms of the activities undertaken for each CKMS device under review.

FR:11.13 The CKMS design **shall** specify the functional and security testing to be performed as part of the periodic security review.

PR:11.9	CA-2	The security of a Federal CKMS **shall** be reviewed annually or in accordance with a Service Level Agreement to assure that it is operating with the latest security updates, incorporating all current CKMS implementer-supported software.

PF:11.2	CA-7	A Federal CKMS **could** perform continuous monitoring of its security-critical key-management processing and data storage capabilities, modules, and devices.

11.3 Incremental Security Assessment

An incremental security assessment is limited in scope and should be conducted after any change is made to the FCKMS that is not a major change to the system or the result of a security compromise (both of which require a full security assessment, as specified in Section 11.1). The scope of the assessment is limited to the specific change involved and any effects that the change could have on the FCKMS performance or security.

116

FR:11.14 The CKMS design **shall** specify the circumstances under which an incremental security assessment should be conducted.

FR:11.15 The CKMS design **shall** specify the scope of incremental security assessments.

PR:11.10	CA-2	A Federal CKMS **shall** undergo an incremental security assessment after any change is made to any part of the FCKMS when the change is not a major change, and the change is not the result of a security compromise.
PR:11.11	CA-2	If a change is major or the result of a security compromise, then a Federal CKMS **shall** undergo a full security assessment as specified in Section 11.1.
PR:11.12		An incremental security assessment for a Federal CKMS **shall** include the identification of any changes to the system since the last security assessment, an architectural review of any design changes, and functional and security testing of the FCKMS.
PR:11.13		A Federal CKMS **shall** support producing a report following an incremental security assessment that includes the following: a) The reasons for any changes; b) Inconsistencies that could have arisen between the CKMS design, the FCKMS implementation, and this Profile; c) The results of the assessment, including all discovered security defects; and d) Any corrective actions to be performed and the dates by which the actions must be completed.

PF:11.3		A Federal CKMS **could** automatically initiate an incremental or full security assessment (as appropriate) after any change to an existing security policy associated with an FCKMS.

11.4 Security Maintenance

While an FCKMS could be designed, implemented, and operated to provide a specific impact-level (e.g., Low, Moderate, or High), the protection provided could be reduced if configuration changes are made or when new threats are identified. In order to maintain or enhance the security of an FCKMS, it should be upgraded in accordance with hardening guidelines (see Section 8.2.1).

FR:11.16 The CKMS design **shall** list the hardening activities required to be performed in order to maintain its security.

PR:11.14	MA-2	Following maintenance activities and before returning to an operational state, the Federal CKMS system administrator **shall**: a) Verify that the security settings are still acceptable, and b) Perform testing against the hardening guidelines in Section 8.2.1 when changes have been made to the FCKMS.

PA:11.8	CA-2	A Federal CKMS **should** support the preparation of a security-assessment report that describes: a) The security maintenance that has been performed on the FCKMS since the last report, b) The current risks of the failure of one or more FCKMS components and/or devices, c) The results of the most recent security assessment, and d) The processes followed in implementing all recommendations for upgrading software or devices that were identified as being subject to failure.
PA:11.9	MA-1 MA-2	A Federal CKMS **should** initiate a security maintenance procedure following notification of an actual or possible security-threatening event.

12 Technological Challenges

A CKMS should be designed and implemented to have a security lifetime of many years. The CKMS designer, FCKMS service provider and the FCKMS service-using organization should periodically evaluate possible threats resulting from advances in technology that may render its key-management services insecure, including[16]:

a) New attacks on cryptographic algorithms,
b) New attacks on key-establishment protocols,
c) New attacks on FCKMS devices, and
d) New computing technologies.

FR:12.1 The CKMS design **shall** specify the expected security lifetime of each cryptographic algorithm implemented in the system.

FR:12.2 The CKMS design **shall** specify which sub-functions (e.g., the hash sub-function of HMAC) of the cryptographic algorithms can be upgraded or replaced with similar, but cryptographically improved, sub-functions without negatively affecting the CKMS operation.

FR:12.3 The CKMS design **shall** specify which key establishment protocols are implemented by the system.

FR:12.4 The CKMS design **shall** specify the expected security lifetime of each key-establishment protocol implemented in the system in terms of the expected security lifetimes of the cryptographic algorithms employed.

FR:12.5 The CKMS design **shall** specify the extent to which external access to CKMS devices is permitted.

FR:12.6 The CKMS design **shall** specify how all allowed external accesses to CKMS devices are controlled.

FR:12.7 The CKMS design **shall** specify the features employed to resist or mitigate the consequences of the development of new technologies, such as a quantum computing attack on the CKMS cryptographic algorithms.

FR:12.8 The CKMS design **shall** specify the currently known consequences of a quantum computing attack upon the CKMS cryptography.

---

[16] See Section 12 of the Framework for detailed descriptions of these threats.

PA:12.1		Throughout the lifetime of a Federal CKMS, the CKMS designer/developer, and the FCKMS service-providing and service-using organizations **should** evaluate possible threats to the FCKMS resulting from advances in technology that may render the FCKMS insecure, including: a) New attacks on cryptographic algorithms, b) New attacks on key-establishment protocols, c) New attacks on FCKMS devices, d) New computing technologies that could reduce the security provided by a cryptographic algorithm, e) New attacks on access control mechanisms, and f) New mathematical attacks that could reduce the protection provided by a cryptographic algorithm and a fixed key length.
PA:12.2		FCKMS management **should** assure that a periodic review of the advances in technology is conducted in order to determine the feasibility and desirability of system improvements.

PF:12.1		Federal CKMS administrators **could** review the current FCKMS technology used in security-domain policy specification, negotiation, and/or enforcement to determine if an upgrade or replacement of the FCKMS is needed.

Appendix A: References

This document references the following publications. All FIPS and NIST Special Publications are available at http://csrc.nist.gov/publications/.

[FIPS 140]   Federal Information Processing Standard (FIPS) 140-2, *Security Requirements for Cryptographic Modules*, May 2001 (with Change Notices through December 3, 2002).
http://csrc.nist.gov/publications/PubsFIPS.html#140-2.

[FIPS 180]   Federal Information Processing Standard (FIPS) 180-4, *Secure Hash Standard*, August 2015.
http://dx.doi.org/10.6028/NIST.FIPS.180-4.

[FIPS 186]   Federal Information Processing Standard (FIPS) 186-4, *Digital Signature Standard (DSS)*, July 2013.
http://dx.doi.org/10.6028/NIST.FIPS.186-4.

[FIPS 197]   Federal Information Processing Standard (FIPS) 197, *Advanced Encryption Standard (AES)*, November 2001.
http://csrc.nist.gov/publications/fips/fips197/fips-197.pdf.

[FIPS 198]   Federal Information Processing Standard (FIPS)198-1, *The Keyed-Hash Message Authentication Code (HMAC)*, July 2008.
http://csrc.nist.gov/publications/fips/fips198-1/FIPS-198-1_final.pdf.

[FIPS 199]   Federal Information Processing Standard (FIPS) 199, *Standards for Security Categorization of Federal Information and Information Systems*, February 2004.
http://csrc.nist.gov/publications/fips/fips199/FIPS-PUB-199-final.pdf.

[FIPS 200]   Federal Information Processing Standard (FIPS) 200, *Minimum Security Requirements for Federal Information and Information Systems*, March 2006.
http://csrc.nist.gov/publications/fips/fips200/FIPS-200-final-march.pdf.

[ISO 19790]   ISO/IEC 19790:2012, *Information technology – Security techniques – Security requirements for cryptographic modules*.
http://www.iso.org/iso/catalogue_detail.htm?csnumber=52906.

[ISO 15408 Parts 1- 3]

ISO/IEC 15408-1:2009, *Information technology -- Security techniques -- Evaluation criteria for IT security -- Part 1: Introduction and general model.*

http://www.iso.org/iso/home/store/catalogue_tc/catalogue_detail.ht
m?csnumber=50341.

ISO/IEC 15408-2:2008, *Information technology -- Security
techniques -- Evaluation criteria for IT security -- Part 2: Security
functional requirements.*
http://www.iso.org/iso/home/store/catalogue_tc/catalogue_detail.ht
m?csnumber=46414.

ISO/IEC 15408-3:2008, *Information technology -- Security
techniques -- Evaluation criteria for IT security -- Part 3: Security
assurance components.*
http://www.iso.org/iso/home/store/catalogue_tc/catalogue_detail.ht
m?csnumber=46413.

[PKCS 1]   Internet Engineering Task Force (IETF) Request for Comment
3447, *Public-Key Cryptography Standard (PKCS) #1: RSA
Cryptography Specifications Version 2.1*, February 2003.
https://www.ietf.org/rfc/rfc3447.txt.

[RFC 5914]   Internet Engineering Task Force (IETF) Request for Comment
5914, *Trust Anchor Format*, June 2010.
https://www.ietf.org/rfc/rfc5914.txt.

[RFC 6024]   Internet Engineering Task Force (IETF) Request for Comment
6024, *Trust Anchor Management Requirements*, October 2010.
https://www.ietf.org/rfc/rfc6024.txt.

[SP 800-37]   NIST Special Publication (SP) 800-37, Revision1, *Guide for
Applying the Risk Management Framework to Federal Information
Systems: A Security Life Cycle Approach*, February 2010.
http://dx.doi.org/10.6028/NIST.SP.800-37r1.

[SP 800-38A]   NIST Special Publication (SP) 800-800-38A, *Recommendation for
Block Cipher Modes of Operation - Methods and Techniques*,
December 2001.
http://csrc.nist.gov/publications/nistpubs/800-38a/sp800-38a.pdf.

[SP 800-38B]   NIST Special Publication (SP) 800-38B, *Recommendation for
Block Cipher Modes of Operation: The CMAC Mode for
Authentication*, May 2005.
http://csrc.nist.gov/publications/nistpubs/800-38B/SP_800-
38B.pdf.

[SP 800-38D]   NIST Special Publication (SP) 800-38D, *Recommendation for
Block Cipher Modes of Operation: Galois/Counter Mode (GCM)
and GMAC*, November 2007.

http://csrc.nist.gov/publications/nistpubs/800-38D/SP-800-38D.pdf.

[SP 800-53]   NIST Special Publication (SP) 800-53 Revision 4, *Security and Privacy Controls for Federal Information Systems and Organizations*, April 2013 (updated January 22, 2015). http://dx.doi.org/10.6028/NIST.SP.800-53r4.

[SP 800-53A]   NIST Special Publication (SP) 800-53A Revision 4, *Guide for Assessing the Security Controls in Federal Information Systems and Organizations, Building Effective Security Assessment Plans*, December 2014. http://dx.doi.org/10.6028/NIST.SP.800-53Ar4.

[SP 800-56A]   NIST Special Publication (SP) 800-56A Revision 2, *Recommendation for Pair-Wise Key-Establishment Schemes Using Discrete Logarithm Cryptography*, May 2013. http://dx.doi.org/10.6028/NIST.SP.800-56Ar2.

[SP 800-56B]   NIST Special Publication (SP) 800-56B Revision 1, *Recommendation for Pair-Wise Key Establishment Schemes Using Integer Factorization Cryptography*, September 2014. http://dx.doi.org/10.6028/NIST.SP.800-56Br1.

[SP 800-57 Part 1] NIST Special Publication (SP) 800-57 Part 1, *Recommendation for Key Management —Part 1: General (Revision 3)*, July 2012. http://csrc.nist.gov/publications/nistpubs/800-57/sp800-57_part1_rev3_general.pdf.

[SP 800-57 Part 3] NIST Special Publication (SP) 800-57 Part 3 Revision 1, *Recommendation for Key Management—Part 3: Application-Specific Key Management Guidance*, January 2015. http://dx.doi.org/10.6028/NIST.SP.800-57pt3r1.

[SP 800-60]   NIST Special Publication (SP) 800-60 Revision 1, *Guide for Mapping Types of Information and Information Systems to Security Categories* [2 vols.], August 2008. http://csrc.nist.gov/publications/PubsSPs.html#800-60.

[SP 800-88]   NIST Special Publication (SP) 800-88 Revision 1, *Guidelines for Media Sanitization*, December 2014. http://dx.doi.org/10.6028/NIST.SP.800-88r1.

[SP 800-89]   NIST Special Publication (SP) 800-89, *Recommendation for Obtaining Assurances for Digital Signature Applications*, November 2006. http://csrc.nist.gov/publications/nistpubs/800-89/SP-800-89_November2006.pdf.

[SP 800-90A]   NIST Special Publication (SP) 800-90A Revision 1,
                    *Recommendation for Random Number Generation Using
                    Deterministic Random Bit Generators*, June 2015.
                    http://dx.doi.org/10.6028/NIST.SP.800-90Ar1.

[SP 800-90B]   Draft NIST Special Publication (SP) 800-90B, *Recommendation
                    for Entropy Sources Used for Random Bit Generation*, August
                    2012 [September 2013].
                    http://csrc.nist.gov/publications/drafts/800-90/draft-sp800-90b.pdf.

[SP 800-90C]   Draft NIST Special Publication (SP) 800-90C, *Recommendation
                    for Random Bit Generator (RBG) Constructions*, August 2012
                    [September 2013].
                    http://csrc.nist.gov/publications/drafts/800-90/draft-sp800-90c.pdf.

[SP 800-108]   NIST Special Publication (SP) 800-108, *Recommendation for Key
                    Derivation Using Pseudorandom Functions*, October 2009.
                    http://csrc.nist.gov/publications/nistpubs/800-108/sp800-108.pdf.

[SP 800-115]   NIST Special Publication (SP) 800-115, *Technical Guide to
                    Information Security Testing and Assessment*, September 2008.
                    http://csrc.nist.gov/publications/nistpubs/800-115/SP800-115.pdf.

[SP 800-126]   NIST Special Publication (SP) 800-126 Rev. 2, *The Technical
                    Specification for the Security Content Automation Protocol
                    (SCAP): SCAP Version 1.2*, September 2011.
                    http://csrc.nist.gov/publications/nistpubs/800-126-rev2/SP800-
                    126r2.pdf.

[SP 800-130]   NIST Special Publication (SP) 800-130, *A Framework for
                    Designing Cryptographic Key Management Systems*, August 2013.
                    http://dx.doi.org/10.6028/NIST.SP.800-130.

[SP 800-131A]   Draft NIST Special Publication (SP) 800-131A Revision 1,
                    *Transitions: Recommendation for Transitioning the Use of
                    Cryptographic Algorithms and Key Lengths*, July 2015.
                    http://csrc.nist.gov/publications/drafts/800-131A/sp800-
                    131a_r1_draft.pdf.

[SP 800-133]   NIST Special Publication (SP) 800-133, *Recommendation for
                    Cryptographic Key Generation*, December 2012.
                    http://dx.doi.org/10.6028/NIST.SP.800-133.

[SP 800-137]   NIST Special Publication (SP) 800-137, *Information Security
                    Continuous Monitoring for Federal Information Systems and
                    Organizations*, September 2011.
                    http://csrc.nist.gov/publications/nistpubs/800-137/SP800-137-
                    Final.pdf.

Appendix B: Glossary

This glossary defines terms that are used in this Profile, some of which may also be defined in the Framework.

Access control system	A set of procedures and/or processes, normally automated, which allows access to a controlled area or to information to be controlled, in accordance with pre-established policies and rules.
Active state	A lifecycle state for a key in which the key may be used to cryptographically protect information (e.g., encrypt plaintext or generate a digital signature), to cryptographically process previously protected information (e.g., decrypt ciphertext or verify a digital signature) or both.
Approved security function	A security function (e.g., cryptographic algorithm, cryptographic key management technique, or authentication technique) that is either a) Specified in an Approved standard, b) Adopted in an Approved standard and specified either in an appendix of the Approved standard or in a document referenced by the Approved standard, or c) Specified in the list of Approved security functions.
Archive	Noun: See _Archive facility_. Verb: To place a cryptographic key and/or metadata into long-term storage that will be maintained even if the storage technology changes.
Archive facility	A facility used for long-term key and/or metadata storage.
Audit log	A record providing documentary evidence of specific events.
Audit administrator	An FCKMS role that is responsible for establishing and reviewing an audit log, assuring that the log is reviewed periodically and after any security-compromise-relevant event, and providing audit reports to FCKMS managers.
Auditor	See _Audit administrator_.
Authorization	The process of verifying that a requested action or service is approved for a specific entity.
Availability	Timely, reliable access to information or a service.
Backup facility	A redundant system or service that is kept available for use in case of a failure of a primary facility.

Backup (key and/or metadata)	To copy a key and/or metadata to a medium that is separate from that used for operational storage and from which the key and/or metadata can be recovered if the original values in operational storage are lost or modified.
Backup (system)	The process of copying information or processing status to a redundant system, service, device or medium that can provide the needed processing capability when needed.
Certification path	A chain of trusted public-key certificates that begins with a certificate whose signature can be verified by a relying party using a trust anchor, and ends with the certificate of the entity whose trust needs to be established.
Ciphertext	Data in its encrypted form.
CKMS	A Cryptographic Key Management System that conforms to the requirements of [SP 800-130].
CKMS design	The capabilities that were selected and specified by a CKMS designer to be implemented and supported in a CKMS product.
CKMS designer	The entity that selects the capabilities to be included in a CKMS, documents the design in accordance with the requirements specified in [SP 800-130], and specifies a CKMS Security Policy that defines the rules that are to be enforced in the CKMS.
CKMS developer	The entity that assembles a CKMS as designed by the CKMS designer.
CKMS implementer	The entity that installs the CKMS for the FCKMS service provider.
CKMS module	A device that performs a set of key and metadata-management functions for at least one CKMS.
CKMS Security Policy	A security policy specific to a CKMS
CKMS product	An implementation of a CKMS design produced by a vendor that conforms to the requirements of [SP 800-130], provides a set of key-management services and cryptographic functions, and operates in accordance with the CKMS designer's CKMS Security Policy.
CKMS vendor	The entity that markets the CKMS to CKMS service providers.
Compatible security domains	Two Security Domains are compatible if they can exchange a key and its metadata without violating (or altering) either domain's FCKMS security policy.

Component	Any hardware, software, and/or firmware required to construct a CKMS.
Compromise (noun)	The unauthorized disclosure, modification, substitution, or use of sensitive data (e.g., keys, metadata, or other security-related information) or the unauthorized modification of a security-related system, device or process in order to gain unauthorized access.
Compromise (verb)	To reduce the trust associated with a key, its metadata, a system, device or process.
Compromise recovery	The procedures and processes of restoring a system, device or process that has been compromised back to a secure or trusted state, including destroying compromised keys, replacing compromised keys (as needed), and verifying the secure state of the recovered system.
Compromised state	A lifecycle state for a key that is known or suspected of being known by an unauthorized entity.
Computer Security Policy	The high-level policy for the security services that are to be supported by a computer for protecting its applications, stored data, and communications, and the rules to be followed in verifying user identities and authorizing their requests before they are granted.
Confidentiality	The property that sensitive information is not disclosed to unauthorized entities.
Configurable	A characteristic of a system, device, or software that allows it to be changed by an entity authorized to select or reject specific capabilities to be included in an operational, configured version.
Copy (data)	To replicate data in another location while maintaining it in its original location.
COTS product	A product that is commercially available.
Cryptographic algorithm	A well-defined computational procedure that takes variable inputs, often including a cryptographic key, and produces an output.

Cryptographic module	The set of hardware, software, and/or firmware that implements security functions (including cryptographic algorithms), holds plaintext keys and uses them for performing cryptographic operations, and is contained within a cryptographic module boundary. This Profile requires the use of a validated cryptographic module as specified in [FIPS 140].
Cryptographic module (compromised)	A cryptographic module whose keys and/or metadata have been subjected to unauthorized access, modification, or disclosure while contained within the cryptographic module.
Cryptographic Module Security Policy	A specification of the security rules under which a cryptographic module is designed to operate.
Cryptographic officer	An FCKMS role that is responsible for and authorized to initialize and manage all cryptographic services, functions, and keys of the FCKMS.
Cryptographic operation	The execution of a cryptographic algorithm. Cryptographic operations are performed in cryptographic modules.
Cryptoperiod	The time span during which a specific key is authorized for use or in which the keys for a given system or application may remain in effect.
Deactivated state	A lifecycle state of a key whereby the key is no longer to be used for applying cryptographic protection. Processing already protected information may still be performed.
Destroyed state	A lifecycle state of a key whereby the key is no longer available and cannot be reconstructed.
Device	A combination of components that function together to serve a specific purpose.
Digital signature	The result of a cryptographic transformation of data that, when properly implemented with a supporting infrastructure and policy, provides the services of: 1. Origin authentication, 2. Data integrity, and 3. Signer non-repudiation.
Domain authority	An FCKMS role that is responsible for determining whether another domain's FCKMS Security Policy is equivalent to or compatible with its own domain policy. The FCKMS system authority often performs this role.
Downgrading	An authorized reduction in the level of protection to be provided to specified information, e.g., from a Moderate impact-level down to a Low impact-level.

Ease-of-use	A metric of satisfaction in using a product as established by one or more individuals using the product.
Entity (party)	An individual (person), organization, device, or process.
Environmental testing	Evaluating the behavior of a device or system to obtain assurance that it will not be compromised by environmental conditions or fluctuations when operating outside the normal environmental operating range.
Equivalent security domains	Two or more security domains that have FCKMS security policies that have been determined to provide equivalent protection for the information.
Error-detection code	A code computed from data and comprised of redundant bits of information that have been designed to detect unintentional changes in the data.
Facility (mobile device)	One or more CKMS devices contained within a physically protected enclosure that is portable (e.g., a mobile phone or a laptop computer). The user of the mobile facility may be required to guard and protect the contents of the facility itself.
Facility (static device)	One or more CKMS devices contained within a physically protected enclosure. A facility for a static device is typically a room or building (including their contents) with locks, alarms, and/or guards.
FCKMS	Federal Cryptographic Key Management System. A CKMS that conforms to the requirements of SP 800-152.
FCKMS (compromised)	An FCKMS whose data have been subjected to unauthorized access, modification, or disclosure while contained within the FCKMS.
FCKMS architecture	The structure of an operational FCKMS, including descriptions and diagrams of the types and locations of all its facilities, FCKMS modules, devices, support utilities, and communications.
FCKMS Component (Component)	Any hardware, software, or firmware that is used to implement an FCKMS.
FCKMS Device (Device)	Any combination of FCKMS components that serve a specific purpose (e.g., firewalls, routers, transmission devices, cryptographic modules, and data storage devices).
FCKMS documentation	The documentation collected or produced by the FCKMS service-providing organization (including the design documentation of the CKMS that will be the foundation of the FCKMS) that states what services and functions are to be provided to FCKMS service-using organizations.

FCKMS functions	Functions that perform cryptographic key and metadata management operations (see Section 6.4 for examples).
FCKMS module	A device that performs a set of key and metadata-management functions for at least one FCKMS and is associated with a cryptographic module. The device may be implemented as hardware, software, and/or firmware.
FCKMS personnel	The individuals of an FCKMS service-providing organization that are authorized to assume the supported roles of the FCKMS.
FCKMS Security Domain	A collection of entities that share a common FCKMS Security Policy
FCKMS Security Policy	A security policy specific to an FCKMS.
FCKMS services (protections)	Protections provided to data, such as data integrity authentication, confidentiality, and source authentication.
FCKMS service provider (FCKMS service-providing organization)	An entity that provides FCKMS key-management services to one or more FCKMS service-using organizations in accordance with their respective FCKMS Security Policies.
FCKMS service-using organization	A Federal organization or contractor that has selected an FCKMS service provider to provide key-management services.
FCKMS Security Policy	The security policy defined by an FCKMS service provider and the FCKMS service-using organization that specifies how the FCKMS will be operated.
FIPS 140 security level	A metric of the security provided by a cryptographic module that is specified as Level 1, 2, 3, or 4, as specified in [FIPS 140], where Level 1 is the lowest level, and Level 4 is the highest level.
Firewall	A part of a computer system or network that is designed to block unauthorized access while permitting outward communication.
Framework (for CKMS)	The CKMS requirements specified in [SP 800-130].
Functional testing	Testing that verifies that an implementation of some function operates correctly.
Hardening	A process intended to eliminate a means of attack by patching vulnerabilities and turning off nonessential services.

Hash function	An algorithm that computes a numerical value (called the hash value) on a data file or electronic message that is used to represent that file or message, and depends on the entire contents of the file or message. A hash function can be considered to be a fingerprint of the file or message.
Impact-level	Refers to the three broadly defined impact-levels in [FIPS 200] that categorize the impact of a security breach as Low, Moderate or High.
Incremental testing	Testing a system or device to determine that minor changes have not affected its security and intended functionality.
Information Management Policy	The high-level policy of an organization that specifies what information is to be collected or created, and how it is to be managed.
Information Security Policy	A high-level policy of an organization that is created to support and enforce portions of the organization's Information Management Policy by specifying in more detail what information is to be protected from anticipated threats and how that protection is to be attained.
Identity-based authentication	A process that provides assurance of an entity's identity by means of an authentication mechanism that verifies the identity of the entity. Contrast with role-based authentication
Integrity	A property whereby data has not been altered in an unauthorized manner since it was created, transmitted, or stored.
Integrity protection	A physical or cryptographic means of providing assurance that information has not been altered in an unauthorized manner since it was created, transmitted, or stored.
Integrity verification	Obtaining assurance that information has not been altered in an unauthorized manner since it was created, transmitted or stored.
Key agreement	A key-establishment procedure where the resultant keying material is a function of information contributed by two or more participants, so that an entity cannot predetermine the resulting value of the keying material independently of any other entity's contribution.
Key confirmation	A procedure to provide assurance to one entity (the key-confirmation recipient) that another entity (the key-confirmation provider) actually possesses the correct secret keying material and/or shared secret.

Key custodian	An FCKMS role that is responsible for distributing keys or key splits and/or entering them into a cryptographic module.
Key derivation	The process of deriving a key in a non-reversible manner from shared information, some of which is secret.
Key distribution	See *Key transport*.
Key establishment	The process that results in the sharing of a key between two or more entities, either by transporting a key from one entity to another (key transport) or generating a key from information shared by the entities (key agreement).
Key format	The data structure of a cryptographic key.
Key life cycle	The period of time between the creation of the key and its destruction.
Key owner	A person authorized by an FCKMS service provider or FCKMS service-using organization to use a specific key that is managed by the FCKMS.
Key (plaintext)	A cryptographic key that can be directly used by a cryptographic algorithm to perform a cryptographic operation.
Key splitting (k of n)	Splitting a key into n key splits so that for some k (where $k \leq n$), any k key splits of the key can be used to form the key, but having any $k-1$ key splits provides no knowledge of the key value.
Key states	A categorization of the states that a key can assume during its lifetime. See [SP 800-57 Part 1].
Key transport	A manual or automated key-establishment procedure whereby one entity (the sender) selects and distributes the key to another entity (the receiver).
Key type	One of the twenty-one types of keys listed in [SP 800-130].
Key update	A key-derivation process whereby the derived key replaces the key from which it was derived when the key-derivation process is later repeated.
Key wrapping	A method of cryptographically protecting keys using a symmetric key that provides both confidentiality and integrity protection.
Key and metadata management functions	Functions performed by a CKMS or FCKMS in order to manage keys and metadata.
Key/metadata recovery	The process of retrieving or reconstructing a key or metadata from backup or archive storage.

Key-recovery agent	An FCKMS role that assists in the key-recovery/metadata-recovery process.
Message Authentication Code (MAC)	A cryptographic checksum on data that uses a symmetric key to detect both accidental and intentional modifications of data.
Malware	Software designed and operated by an adversary to violate the security of a computer (includes spyware, virus programs, root kits, and Trojan horses).
Message authentication	A process that provides assurance of the integrity of messages, documents or stored data.
Metadata (explicit)	Parameters used to describe the properties associated with a cryptographic key that are explicitly recorded, managed, and protected by the CKMS.
Metadata (implicit)	Information about a cryptographic key that may be inferred (i.e., by context), but is not explicitly recorded, managed, or protected by the CKMS.
Metadata (bound)	Metadata that has been cryptographically combined with the associated key to produce a MAC or digital signature that can be used to verify that the key and metadata are indeed associated with each other.
Metadata (compromised)	Sensitive metadata that has been disclosed to or modified by an unauthorized entity.
Multi-level security domain	A security domain that supports information protection at more than one impact-level.
NIST-allowed	Specified in a list of allowed security functions (e.g., in an annex to [FIPS 140]).
NIST-approved	FIPS-approved or NIST-Recommended.
Operating system	A collection of software that manages computer hardware resources and provides common services for computer programs.
Operational storage	Storage within an FCKMS where the key can be accessed to perform cryptographic functions during normal operations.
Operator	An FCKMS role that is authorized to operate an FCKMS (e.g., initiate the FCKMS, monitor performance, and perform backups), as directed by the system administrator.
Parameter	A value that is used to control the operation of a function or that is used by a function to compute one or more outputs.
Party	See Entity.

Penetration testing	Testing that verifies the extent to which a system, device or process resists active attempts to compromise its security.
Personal accountability	A policy that requires that every person who accesses sensitive information be held accountable for his or her actions. A method for identity authentication is required.
Personnel-security compromise	The accidental or intentional action of any person that reduces the security of the FCKMS and/or compromises any of its keys and sensitive metadata.
Physical-security compromise	The unauthorized access to sensitive data, hardware, and/or software by physical means.
Pre-activation state	A lifecycle state of a key in which the key has been created, but is not yet authorized for use.
Primary facility	An FCKMS facility that houses a primary system.
Primary system	An FCKMS module that is currently active. Contrast with Backup (system).
Private key	A cryptographic key used by a public-key (asymmetric) cryptographic algorithm that is uniquely associated with an entity and is not made public.
Profile (for a CKMS)	A document that provides an implementation-independent specification of CKMS security requirements for use by a community of interest (e.g., U.S. Government, banking, health, or aerospace).
Profile (for an FCKMS)	The specifications for Federal CKMSs in SP 800-152, including the requirements for their design, implementation, procurement, installation, configuration, management, operation, and use by Federal organizations and their contractors
Profile augmentations	The properties or characteristics that are recommended, but not required, by this Profile for FCKMSs.
Profile features	The properties or characteristics that **could** be used by FCKMSs, but are not required or recommended by this Profile.
Profile requirements	The properties or characteristics that **shall** be exhibited in FCKMSs in order to conform to, or comply with, this Profile.
Public key	A cryptographic key used by a public-key (asymmetric) cryptographic algorithm that may be made public.
Registration agent	An FCKMS role that is responsible for registering new entities and perhaps other selected information.

Relying party	In this Recommendation, a party that relies on the security and authenticity of a key or key pair for applying cryptographic protection and removing or verifying the protection that has been applied. This includes parties relying on the public key in a public key certificate and parties that share a symmetric key.
Role-based authentication	A process that provides assurance of an entity's role by means of an authentication mechanism that verifies the role of the entity. Contrast with identity-based authentication
Scalability testing	Testing the ability of a system to handle an increasing amount of work correctly.
Secret key	A cryptographic key used by a secret-key (symmetric) cryptographic algorithm and that is not made public.
Security assessment	An evaluation of the security provided by a system, device or process.
Security strength	A number associated with the expected amount of work (that is, the base 2 logarithm of the number of operations) to cryptanalyze a cryptographic algorithm or system.
Security testing	Testing that attempts to verify that an implementation protects data and maintains functionality as intended.
Self testing	Testing within a system, device or process during normal operation to detect misbehavior.
Semantics	The intended meaning of acceptable sentences of a language.
Sentences, formal	The entire set of sentences that can be created or recognized as being valid using the formal syntax specifications of a formal language.
Service Level Agreement (SLA)	A service contract between an FCKMS service provider and an FCKMS service-using organization that defines the level of service to be provided, such as the time to recover from an operational failure or a system compromise.
Source authentication	A process that provides assurance of the source of information.
Store a key or metadata	Placing a key and/or metadata in storage outside of a cryptographic module without retaining the original copy in the cryptographic module.
Support	To be capable of providing a service or perform a function that is required or desired; to agree with a policy or position; to fulfill requirements.

Suspended state	A lifecycle state of a key whereby the use of the key for applying cryptographic protection has been temporarily suspended.
Semantics of a language	The meanings of all the language's acceptable sentences.
Symmetric key	See *Secret key*.
Syntax	The rules for constructing or recognizing the acceptable sentences of a language.
System administrator	An FCKMS role that is responsible for the personnel, daily operation, training, maintenance, and related management of an FCKMS other than its keys. The system administrator is responsible for initially verifying individual identities, and then establishing appropriate identifiers for all personnel involved in the operation and use of the FCKMS.
System authority	An FCKMS role that is responsible to executive-level management (e.g., the Chief Information Officer) for the overall operation and security of an FCKMS. A system authority manages all operational FCKMS roles.
Third-party testing	Independent testing by an organization that was not involved in the design and implementation of the object being tested (e.g., a system or device) and is not intended as the eventual user of that object.
Trust	A characteristic of an entity that indicates its ability to perform certain functions or services correctly, fairly and impartially, along with assurance that the entity and its identifier are genuine.
Trust anchor	A CA with one or more trusted certificates containing public keys that exist at the base of a tree of trust or as the strongest link in a chain of trust and upon which a Public Key Infrastructure is constructed. "Trust anchor" also refers to the certificate of this CA.
Trusted channel	A protected communication link established between the cryptographic module and a sender or receiver (including another cryptographic module) to securely communicate and verify the validity of plaintext CSPs, keys, authentication data, and other sensitive data. Also called a secure channel.
Trusted (secure) operating system	An operating system that manages data to make sure that it cannot be altered, moved, or viewed except by entities having appropriate and authorized access rights.

Upgrading	An authorized increase in the level of protection to be provided to specified information, e.g., from a Low impact-level to a Moderate impact-level.
User	An FCKMS role that utilizes the key-management services offered by an FCKMS service provider.
User interface	The physical or logical means by which users interact with a system, device or process.
Validation	The process of determining that an object or process is acceptable according to a pre-defined set of tests and the results of those tests.